JESUS IN CONTEXT

Why a Jewish Jesus Matters to Christian Believers

By Doron Katz with Paul Edwards

TABLE OF CONTENTS

JESUS IN CONTEXT

Why a Jewish Jesus Matters to Christian Believers

© 2024 Doron Katz & Paul Edwards

Emissary
PUBLISHING

ISBN 979-8-9905562-3-2
Published in Phoenix, Arizona by Emissary Publishing.
Emissary is a business trade name of Ed's Voices, LLC.
Scripture quotations are taken from the following sources:
The Complete Jewish Bible by David H. Stern. Copyright © 1998.
All rights reserved. Used by permission of Messianic Jewish Publishers, 6120 Day Long Lane, Clarksville, MD 21029.
www.messianicjewish.net.

The NIV Bible (The Holy Bible, New International Version), Copyright 1978 by Biblica Ministries, a nonprofit Bible and publishing ministry.

INTRODUCTION

What you're about to read is one of the "best-kept open secrets" of all time.

We proceed with cautious humility and encourage you to do the same. This is an attempt to move away from a significant degree of speculation, according to historical and presumptive Western understandings, about the man known to most Westerners as Jesus Christ, the Son of God—the central figure of Western civilization and the Christian religion, in all its various denominations and subcategories.

This book represents a departure from books we have read in attempts to understand this man. We declare so unreservedly, with complete confidence, aware that most attempts by modern Christians to investigate and more thoroughly understand Jesus are subject to a self-imposed, unconscious bias. It is a bias taught silently by some teachers (and not others) in every denomination (at least, throughout Western Christendom) to varying degrees. By definition, according to doctrines and disciplines we have read in all three major branches of Christianity (Catholic, Protestant, and Orthodox), the 3500 years' worth of Jewish history, theological study, and debate that preceded, surrounded, and lingered from Jesus' ascension well into the present day … must be (at best) marginalized and diminished, and (at worst) rejected and excluded from serious theological study or application.

This tradition stretches back to the waning days of the apostolic era and the spread of Christianity across Europe. At first blush, its effects might seem benign and inconsequential, particularly if you're a Gentile. For example, if you view Jewish activities like observing the Sabbath on Saturday as "neither here nor there," you might not attach much significance to efforts by early Christians (like the Roman emperor Constantine) to change or abolish them.[1] Whether such efforts were "evil" or "malicious" is beside the point; regardless of the intent, the result is the exclusion and silencing of the moral and intellectual underpinnings of the New Testament, which Jesus himself quoted and discussed at great length.

The Council of Nicea, convened by Roman emperor Constantine in 325 A.D., rejected and excluded Jewish tradition. In speaking of the Christian tradition of Easter, the emperor said, "We ought not, therefore, to have anything in common with the Jews ... [but] to separate ourselves from the detestable company of the Jews, for it is truly shameful for us to hear them boast that without their direction we could not keep this feast."

In some instances, we venture that certain Gentile believers in Jesus went beyond rejecting Jewish tradition or influence and rose to the level of contradicting the Bible itself. In the case of the Sabbath, which is made permanent (forever) by God himself to Moses in Exodus,[2] no subsequent verse directs Jews or Christians to alter it to Sunday.

---

[1] https://www.icej.org/blog/the-breach-where-the-church-parted-ways-with-israel/

[2] Exodus 31:14-17

This bias persisted through the Middle Ages and into the Renaissance, on the tongues of church fathers like Eusebius,[3] Bishop of Caesarea Maritima, and famous Christian preachers like John Chrysostom.[4] Both of these men made statements that discouraged Christians from observing the traditional seventh-day Sabbath and (in Chrysostom's case) uttered curses and defamations against the Jews that resonated among Europeans well into the Medieval period.

Nine hundred years after these statements, the Fourth Lateran Council of the Catholic Church convened by Pope Innocent in 1215 required Jews throughout Christendom to wear badges to identify themselves and forbade Jewish converts to Christianity from "retaining their old rite" (i.e., observing Jewish traditions in the practice of their new faith).[5] A decade or so later, the Spanish Inquisition took this antipathy to a new level – they offered Jews the choice of converting to Catholicism or exile from Spain.[6] Two centuries after that, Pope Paul IV established a Jewish "ghetto" in Rome and published the doctrine *Extra Ecclesiam Nulla Salus*, which translates to "There is no salvation outside the

---

[3] Guy, Laurie (4 November 2004). *Introducing Early Christianity: A Topical Survey of Its Life, Beliefs and Practices*. InterVarsity Press. p. 213. ISBN 9780830826988. Significantly, the first Christian writer to suggest that the Sabbath had been transferred to Sunday is Eusebius of Caesarea (post 330).

[4] https://www.worldhistory.org/article/2337/christian-antisemitism-in-the-middle-ages--during/

[5] https://www.worldhistory.org/article/2337/christian-antisemitism-in-the-middle-ages--during/

[6] https://en.wikipedia.org/wiki/Expulsion_of_Jews_from_Spain

(Catholic) church." Naturally, this excluded Judaism from the conversation.

The hostility toward Jews and Judaism of certain leaders of the Protestant Reformation, most notably Martin Luther himself, is well-documented and (to their credit) acknowledged by modern Protestant and Lutheran theologians and the churches they lead.[7] In his 1543 essay *On the Jews and Their Lies*, Luther called (among other things) for "the prohibition of the teaching and practice of their religion."

It has only been in the last few centuries that prejudice toward Jewish commentary and history has slowly come into focus among certain preachers and leaders throughout Christendom, and Christian institutions have gradually relaxed doctrines they previously clung to regarding the validity of Jewish scholarship and context.

Among the famous Pilgrims who landed in the New World in Plymouth, Massachusetts, in 1620 was the future governor of Plymouth Plantation, William Bradford. In the pages of his famous journal, *On Plymouth Plantation*, you can find over 1000 Hebrew words, phrases, and definitions.[8] Jonathan Edwards, famous among Americans for his sermon "Sinners In the Hands of an Angry God," predicted the return of the Jews to the land of Israel and

---

[7] https://www.christianitytoday.com/history/issues/issue-39/was-luther-anti-semitic.html

[8] https://evengilion.org/the-man-who-brought-hebrew-to-america/

their eventual repentance for rejecting Jesus as Messiah.[9] Many American universities founded by Christians in the 18th and 19th Centuries, including famous ones like Yale,[10] taught Hebrew to their students.

As the Industrial Revolution gave way to the modern era, openness from Christians toward Jews and Judaism improved in fits and starts. In the late 19th Century, Christian Zionists joined forces with Jews in advocating and working for a reestablishment of a Jewish homeland.[11] Fifty years later, American President Harry Truman, who was raised in a devout Christian home, overruled the hostile United Nations and a reticent Great Britain into accepting the modern State of Israel.[12] After Israel recaptured Jerusalem in 1967, the Catholic Church became the first major branch of Christianity to renounce and repudiate its former hostility toward the Jewish people through the *Nostra Aetate* declaration.[13]

Few would argue that the clash between Judaism and Christianity is less violent today than it once was. Our experience, however, along with simple research examining sermons, written

---

[9] https://www.sermonindex.net/modules/newbb/viewtopic.php?topic_id=26875&forum=35

[10] https://www.jewishvirtuallibrary.org/how-hebrew-came-to-yale

[11] https://fathomjournal.org/british-christian-zionism-and-george-eliots-daniel-deronda/

[12] https://www.shapell.org/manuscript/truman-israel-independence-war/?gad_source=1&gclid=CjwKCAjw1emzBhB8EiwAHwZZxdAifQtJSPzy4IE EgdPrEs44w1COYH6MtGD95XZxYuSCe72UA27FfBoCmIcQAvD_BwE

[13] https://en.wikipedia.org/wiki/Nostra_aetate

teachings, and literature online from prominent Christian preachers – seems to reinforce a "code of silence" on Jewish perspective and extrabiblical content. By and large, most Christians we've ever spoken to know almost nothing about Jewish texts like the *Talmud*, the *Mishnah,* or apocryphal texts like *Maccabees* and *Enoch.* At churches both of us have attended (predominantly evangelical Protestant congregations), teachers occasionally pause to translate Hebrew words … but Jewish writings and explanations remain entirely muted. Among more scholarly and renowned Christian thinkers, we sometimes hear detailed expositions of background and context. But with equal regularity, we listen to teachings that show adherence to the notion that Judaism must be (at best) marginalized and diminished and (at worst) rejected and excluded. If not explicitly stated, it is left in silence by the theology of supersessionism, also known as "replacement theology."[14]

To be clear, neither of us has ever heard a Christian preacher directly say, "You must reject Jews and Judaism and never associate with them because they are heretics." On the contrary, most churches and Christians we know support Israel's right to exist, pray regularly for, and make public statements honoring the Jewish people. At the same time, however, we have heard several preachers and lay leaders speak dismissively of the Old Testament as "the old law" or tell us to ignore certain parts of Scripture because "that's Jewish stuff you don't need to worry about."

---

[14] https://en.wikipedia.org/wiki/Supersessionism

It would be fine if those same preachers had not also told us things like, "You need to read every word of your Bible because it's all for you." Those two statements contradict each other.

Ironically, it is these Jewish writings, meditations, and annals of history that contain the "clues" most Christians would be eager to learn as they wrestle with a library of texts that often seems repetitive, incoherent, random, and anachronistic (not to mention, full of apparent contradictions). We regularly observe a hunger and enthusiasm among Christians when we share Judaism's perspective on the Scriptures they read. The hunger they display lends weight to the notion that in their zeal for rescuing the lost, churches have (inadvertently) malnourished the "found." Aware of concepts like Jesus "leaving the 99 to rescue the one," we do not see additional text directing leaders to *neglect* the 99 or take them for granted.

In the meantime, where else can we look? The clues to the reality of Jesus as the Jewish Messiah are not to be found among the writings and lore of any other ancient civilization. Jesus is not a figure of literature or folklore from ancient Babylon, ancient Rome, ancient Greece, ancient China, or any other civilization that existed at the time. Nothing can be found in the relics and preserved writings of those societies that lends any credibility or insight into who he is or what made his life so significant that to this day, we organize the Western calendar around his birth.

Yet Jesus is nothing if he is not a Jew, a citizen of Israel, the son of Jewish parents, the grandson of Jewish ancestors, the descendant of Jewish kings, who grew up in Jewish communities surrounded by Jewish neighbors, Jewish businesses, Jewish synagogues, and Jewish priests and rabbis. We shut ourselves off from a great deal of context if we take Jesus for anything other than a man who preached a Jewish message to Jewish disciples and Jewish audiences using the Jewish Scriptures as his theological and ethical foundation. He was a master theologian who debated publicly with top Jewish rabbis and scholars about interpretations of those Jewish Scriptures (written exclusively in the biblical Hebrew language) and who, on numerous occasions, proclaimed himself the fulfillment, embodiment, and supreme authority on the **Torah**. Known to most Christians as "The Old Testament," the Torah is the central authoritative document of Jewish life. (*In traditional Judaism, the Torah contains every book from Genesis to Malachi; for Messianic Jews, it also includes the New Testament.*)

In his debates and sermons, Jesus quoted strictly from the Jewish Scriptures; he did not cite the New Testament (as it did not yet exist), nor did he refer to the Code of Hammurabi, the wisdom of Confucius, or the works of philosophers in Athens or Rome. He never invoked the Muslim Qu'ran, the Hindu Bhagavad Gita, or Buddhist or Taoist texts. He neither proclaimed himself nor was he mocked or crucified as "King of the Romans" or "King of the Mesopotamians." The only title he seriously entertained was King of the *Jews*. We believe this reluctance toward and avoidance of his Jewish identity hampers his followers from more fully understanding him. It is time to stop pretending he was someone or something other than what he was. This itinerant Jewish rabbi lived exclusively in the land of Israel, speaking Hebrew and Aramaic and interacting almost exclusively with other Jews.

Stop and think for a moment: Would we treat any other document of that age with such casual disregard for its culture and context? For example, a study of an ancient document like *The Iliad* dutifully recognizes its Greekness—its Greek author, protagonist, and polytheistic worldview. We read, for example, that Odysseus drew his bow and said, "Help me, Apollo." Do we then think, for even a moment, that he was secretly a medieval Viking who worshiped Thor?

Likewise, when we read *The Art of War* by legendary Chinese general Sun-Tzu, we do not forsake his Chinese-ness. Do we *learn* great ideas and find profound philosophical quotes from these works? Absolutely! But do we then pretend that Sun-Tzu thought of 21st Century Westerners when he wrote his book? Of course not. We never subsume these works or their authors as "blank canvases" onto which we can project our biases, assumptions, and realities. At worst, it would be a common intellectual courtesy to afford the same humility and openness to the Bible.

This is what makes Jesus' Jewishness a dividing line. Unlike *The Odyssey* or *The Art of War*, billions of Christians seek to organize their entire lives, families, careers, social circles, and societal structures around an extremely Jewish library, written from end to end by Jews, to Jews, and (predominantly) for Jews. You can write off Homer's Greekness or Sun-Tzu's Chineseness all you want, without consequence, because you're not trying to live as an "Odyssean" or a Sun-Tzu practitioner. You don't even have to read their books.

But Jesus is different, particularly if you claim to believe he is who he says he is. It is intellectually possible to exclude his identity from his teachings ... but as a practical matter, it's unwise.

As with any other attempt to study Jesus, over 2000 years since his death and resurrection, we must first acknowledge the elephant in the room: none of us were physically alive, much less privileged to travel in his inner circle when he walked the earth. We can make calculated assumptions about what he said and did based on a detailed understanding of what his rhetoric and exchanges are *likely* to have meant ... but we never know for sure, as though we have film or transcript evidence. Even if that were the case, we should acknowledge that understanding him often resembles the children's game of "Telephone" – one of us would hear one thing, while the next would hear something else.

We'd also be fools to speculate on what Jesus said and did that is <u>not</u> recorded. Just because he shows up one way in one recorded instance does not mean he operated that same way in every instance before or after that. When we encounter him in eternity, we expect to be pleasantly surprised by all the stories we've *never* heard because they weren't written down or recorded.

This reinforces the question – isn't it dangerous to "make up" things Jesus never said or did? Are we not warned, at the end of Revelation, that "if anyone adds anything to what is written here, God will add to him the plagues described in this book"?[15]

---

[15] Revelation 22:18

Don't we owe it to God to restrain ourselves from fanciful reflections about how he *might* have behaved or spoken … when, with practice and good teaching, we can instead focus on how he *usually* behaved and spoke, to the extent the apostles recorded it in writing?

But even then, we'd also be fools to try restraining or confining the God of Israel. We readily acknowledge that he can behave or speak however he pleases. Sometimes, he does just that.

It seems wiser to study what he *reveals* about himself versus what he conceals.

In that spirit, we preface everything you're about to read with the caveat:

"We are already wrong, to some degree, in some way of which we are not yet aware."

And we're okay with that. After all these centuries, it seems God is okay with it, too. He retains the final word and knows the whole truth of every matter. He reserves the right to let us fumble about with our attempts to understand him … and simultaneously rewards us for sincerely pursuing them. He does want to be known, but as the psalmist wrote in Psalm 18:26, he's in no hurry to be known by people who cannot fully appreciate him: "To the pure, you show yourself pure; but to the wicked, you show yourself shrewd."

God is content to conceal himself from people hostile or opposed to him or his kingdom. Perhaps we should consider that before we dismiss his national identity – because he does have one.

Unlike any modern Gentile nation, there is one nation with whom he *does* have a written covenant: the nation of Israel. According to the apostle he appointed to the Gentiles (Paul), we who are Gentiles are "grafted" into their spiritual commonwealth.[16]

Everything we're about to expose has a <u>Scriptural</u>, rather than a purely speculative, underpinning. Some of what we present is speculative, but only to the extent it remains reconcilable with Scripture. We make some assumptions about what Jesus said and did, but only based on knowledge of Jewish culture, customs, and context. We do not make assertions or suggestions that contradict or undermine the Word of God. If you're familiar with the award-winning streaming series *The Chosen*, this series will use the same sort of liberties: imagination within the boundaries of Scripture.

For a brief example of what we mean by "pure speculation," consider this treatment we have heard from the mouth of a Christian preacher about the apostles Peter and John during the second miraculous catch of fish recorded in John's Gospel,[17] following Jesus' resurrection:

"John recorded the miraculous catch of 153 fish because he and Peter were competitive fishermen who liked to write down who caught the most fish."

At best, such an interpretation is baseless speculation; no evidence or literature supports it. There *is* a reasonable tendency to assume that young Jewish men in their late teens and early

---

[16] Romans 11:11-31

[17] John 21:1-14

twenties, as Peter and John were, would be competitive toward each other. To a casual modern observer, that may seem entirely feasible. However, John records the number of 153 fish for an altogether different, mystical, and profoundly Jewish reason — one only a particular audience of desert-dwelling Jewish mystics would notice or understand. (Lest you wonder, that reason will come to light in this book's sequel, *The Gospel In Context*.)

Like Sun-Tzu, John had no idea that 2000 years later, English-speaking Westerners would assume he and Peter were the equivalents of competitive frat boys who wanted to "one-up" each other. Nor would it have likely occurred to him to insert such detail when elsewhere he wrote that "these things are written down so that you may believe that Jesus is the Son of God."[18]

Instead, John wrote in real-time to a group of people he knew, the same way the rest of the Bible's authors did. Can you find any corresponding competitive banter in the gospel of Mark, which is traditionally attributed to Peter, or in either of Peter's letters, where Peter takes affectionate "shots" at John? No.

This doesn't mean the pastor we quoted was spreading heresy. Instead, it means he's making his best-educated guess ... but his guess is problematic because it excludes Judaism, replacing it with 21st-Century platitudes.

If this scenario were a group of friends idly bantering about who would win in a battle between fictional characters like the Incredible Hulk and Darth Vader, speculation would be fine. We

---

[18] John 20:31

both enjoy the nonsensical "How it should have ended" video series on YouTube. Human imagination is powerful and tends to "fill in the gaps" when parts of a story are left blank or unexplained.

But when pastors expect congregants to take them seriously, follow their instructions, and submit to their authority as the first line of biblical mediation between God and man, we should all do our homework, pastors and laypersons alike. And we should not exclude Judaism.

So, let's dig a little deeper.

Early on, we'll paint the picture of who Jesus truly was based on what a First Century Jewish audience would have likely assumed when they encountered him and listened to what he taught. We'll also delve into what that same audience would likely have thought when they heard stories about him or read the gospels and letters of the apostles. While it is important to wonder and reconstruct what non-Jewish believers would have thought when they received the message … it is unproductive and inauthentic to exclude the Jewish response for the simple reason that most of the people who heard Jesus speak were fellow Jews.

From there, we will take a good, hard look at what is written about Jesus. You'll see numerous cases of why it is counterproductive to read about him in a one-dimensional, literal interpretation of the Hebrew and Greek texts and "retroject" 21st Century Western culture and customs onto him. You'll learn, through examples from the Hebrew Scriptures and what is commonly called the "New Testament," why you can't afford to read the Bible the way you would read a modern biography or manifesto.

We'll spend time exploring some of Jesus' words and sayings. Nowhere is he more misunderstood than by his own words, and chapters 3-5 deal extensively with things he said, what he meant by them, and what his audiences are likely to have understood when they heard it. We'll take apart some of the most famous narratives we've heard about him throughout the Western churches we've visited and delve into aspects of his personality he is not supposed to have had, according to church tradition: sarcasm, ridicule, insults, and gruffness. (Yes, he did have them.)

We'll demonstrate to you, verbally and visually, how we arrive at our conclusions. We'll review several passages that appear "random," even unnecessary or frivolous until viewed through Jewish eyes and on the biblical timeline and template.

Throughout our time together, we pray that you learn to reconcile and settle in your mind everything we teach through the lens of Scriptural authority, followed by the weightiness of commentary and supporting works. In an ironic twist, the New Testament leans on extra-biblical Jewish literature for several of its arguments. On that precept, we feel comfortable doing no more and no less — provided the latter never contradicts or supersedes the former. Our philosophy, in entertaining the legends and teachings of Ancient Jewish Wisdom, goes something like this:

(A) If it fulfills, points to, or aligns with the identity of Jesus as the Son of God, the promised Jewish Messiah, and the Source of Eternal Salvation;

and

(B) If it can be directly or plausibly reconciled to the supreme, central authority of the Hebrew Scriptures, the Gospels, and the Writings of the Apostles …

… then it is entirely within the realm of possibility, especially if doing so enhances the argument for Jesus' candidacy as Messiah to the Jewish people, as well as to Gentiles.

Although Scripture never contradicts itself, we greatly respect modern Western readers' limitations. There are, to be sure, several passages that *appear* to do just that—contradict other passages—and we regard it as our solemn obligation to dig deep into the language, context, background, and cultural setting of those passages so that we might assist modern believers in properly discerning the meaning and substance of what they read.

The alternative is unacceptable — sincere and eager disciples, reading and inferring ideas and concepts we were never meant to entertain or contemplate, much less use them as a pretext to detract from the mission of bringing light, peace, and joy into the world.

With as much respect as we have for biblical scholarship and traditional religious educational programs, such as seminaries or divinity schools, we politely and firmly disagree with any assertion that we are "unqualified" to speak or write on this subject. The message you are about to read is born of *lingering, suffocating, and frustrating pain* from years and decades of longing to engage and respond to the God of Israel and his son …

yet feeling like the more we studied and applied it, the less we understood. Pain from dutifully reading and studying the Scriptures, on the direction of Christian pastors, only to find lengthy portions and passages that made no rational or literary sense, offered little to nothing in the way of inspiration, and (in some cases) seemed to lay down examples that backfired when we tried to implement them in real life.

It's also worth noting at the outset, as we'll repeat at turns, that we haven't got room to account for <u>every</u> Christian belief or interpretation of what they read and study. You may encounter statements that sound like sweeping generalizations, to which you may react by thinking, "I don't believe that, and neither does my pastor." For that, we can only say that this book describes what *we have observed* through personal interactions and online media, for anyone interested enough to look and listen carefully.

One of us is a Messianic Jewish rabbi who has spent the last decade ministering primarily to disaffected Christians, from one denomination to the next. The other was a Christian for 18 years, educated mainly through Catholic and evangelical Protestant theology, who became a Messianic Gentile who still "caucuses" with evangelical Christians and attends Sunday services. This is most definitely the work of two men who spend a <u>lot</u> of time in churches, around Christians, and serving in various ministries. It would be impossible to take either of our journeys and <u>not</u> encounter dogma, doctrine, or assertions that dismiss or deride Judaism.

So, concerning *individual* Christian beliefs, we only ask that "if the shoe fits, wear it." If your belief aligns with ours, we applaud you; if it doesn't, it's entirely your business what you do with it. We do not view ourselves as responsible for your salvation, nor do we subscribe to any notion or dogma that tells outsiders, "You're going to hell if you don't believe what we believe." We worship a God who can clear things up when and where he chooses – including with us if we're wrong.

You can argue, in other words, that we lack degrees in biblical studies from accredited postmodern Western academies or seminaries; you cannot argue the pain, sorrow, and loneliness either of us felt as we misinterpreted and fumbled about with vague, diminished applications of what we read and studied. You can disqualify us from sitting on the preeminent boards and institutions of biblical scholarship; you cannot write off our shared experiences as mere figments of vanity and imagination. *Especially* when our attempts to live the Christian experience accorded with the teaching we absorbed from men trained by those same postmodern Western academies – and failed to produce the fruit we were promised.

So let us move, as the epistle to the Hebrews says, beyond the elementary teachings concerning Jesus … by first returning to them. We will take them apart and put them back together to better understand and respond to them.

We hope and believe that our work spurs you into the truest, deepest, and most settled understanding of who Jesus was, is, and will be when he returns.

- Doron Katz & Paul Edwards

CHAPTER ONE
The Child: Identity Markers in Scripture

In 2010, along with my brother, I (Doron) took a guided trip through many of the Biblical sites in Israel. We enjoyed following our tour guide, a native Israeli who shared detailed knowledge of each site we visited. Of all the things he shared, one statement he made, particularly for the Christians who joined us on the tour, may have been completely lost on them. He lowered his voice, focused his gaze, and said, "I don't want to shock you, but Jesus was not born with blond hair and blue eyes."

Of course, all the Christians who were present laughed. But I don't think they grasped the rebuke concealed within the comment. Judging by their reactions, it was a subtle distinction, a mere historical triviality that mattered as much as any other historical detail. Up to that point, I'd received the same teaching on Jesus' nationality, more or less from the same perspective as anyone else. I attached no significance to his Jewish identity, even though I am a Jew. But if you've ever taken a trip to Israel to learn more about your faith, you likely realized that our "Western Makeover Edition" of Jesus is problematic.

Another thing that stood out was the fact that our Jewish guide felt the need to "ask permission" from Christians to call Jesus by His actual Hebrew name, "Yeshua," as opposed to the Gentile, Greco-English "Jesus." That moment confirmed for me that we have an identity problem; for the last 1700 years, we've tried to rebrand a Jewish man into a non-Jewish one, and we have succeeded. For a Jew, there is a discomfort inherent in calling

Jesus by his real name, as if he is "on loan" to them from Gentile Christianity — when, in fact, the truth is precisely the opposite. In his own words, the Son of God was (and is) as Jewish as they come. Because of his profound goodness and generosity, he opened the gates of his coming kingdom to Gentiles.

Why Mention Jesus' Circumcision?

To see people strip Jesus of His native Hebrew identity, purely out of habit, reminds me of what I've heard spoken in many churches: the Hebrew Bible (Old Testament) — along with its traditions, commentary, and indeed, the Jewish people themselves — are (at best) obsolete and irrelevant to the "new" agenda of God. And as long as believers continue to read the writings in the New Testament without a Jewish perspective, this upside-down narrative prominent in Christian circles remains plausible and accepted.

Only when we insist on understanding why these passages exist and what they mean do some common Christian interpretations and doctrines crumble and collapse. There's no need to fear letting go of Christian doctrine; it's only a bad idea if it undermines Scripture. If doctrines lack God's official stamp of approval and authority in the Bible ... we have no more to fear in reforming or abolishing them than when the Catholic Church published *Nostra Aetate* and renounced their past antisemitism. False doctrines abound in Christianity, whichever denomination you follow.

But as for the Word of our God ... it endures forever, as the Proverbs say.[19] It is eternal, unchanging, relevant, and valuable throughout every epoch and era of human history. If this is true, we must ask — is there another way to examine the connection between the Hebrew Bible and the writings of Jesus' apostles? If so, does such a perspective align with the supreme authority of Scripture? Would it undermine the authority of the gospels to look at them as *continuations* rather than declarations of independence from the Hebrew Bible?

Some passages require close examination and reflection because they appear to create or reinforce the presumed separation. If everything in Scripture were crystal clear to all human beings throughout every epoch of history, endless arguments among Jews and Christians would never happen. But as we Jews joke among ourselves, "If nine out of ten people agree on something, that means the tenth person is Jewish!" And you could just as easily substitute Christians in there as well.

Let's begin with something simple from Luke, the disciple best known for his talents as a historian, who noted the following concerning Jesus' birth:

"On the eighth day, when it was time to circumcise the child, he was named Jesus, the name the angel had given him before he was conceived. And when the time came for their purification according to the Law of Moses, they brought him up to Jerusalem to present him to the Lord."[20]

---

[19] Isaiah 40:8

[20] Luke 2:21-22

This passage addresses the misconception of some kind of "divide" between the Old and New Testaments. Here, Gentile believers should pause and ponder the implication of Jesus' parents dedicating the Messiah under Old Testament practices. Circumcision is more than a longstanding Jewish tradition; it is also a mark that identifies the bearer as a member of the nation of Israel. It dates back to Abraham, before the giving of the Torah on Mount Sinai, and before the Jewish nation was formed.[21] Later, in the writings of Paul to the believers in Galatia, circumcision became a point of contention for precisely this reason: Gentile believers who underwent circumcision forsook their identity as Gentiles and became "naturalized" Israelites. For Jesus' parents to circumcise him meant that he was, inextricably, a member of the nation of Israel. A Jew, if ever there was one.

As a Gentile Christian for 18 years, I (Paul) typically wrote this passage off as a nondescript narrative every time I read it. In milliseconds I would think, "Well, that's what everyone did in those days. Jesus' parents were just following the rules. He hadn't lived his life yet, so that's fine. Circumcision complete. Good! Done and dusted, checked the box. Move along; nothing to see here."

I had no idea circumcision was a mark of nationality, and no pastor I listened to ever mentioned it ...

---

[21] Genesis 17:9-14

... but it's in there!

You might wonder what all the fuss is about. "So what? It's in there; we've read it, and let's move on."

Here's why that's problematic.

During those 18 years in evangelical circles, I heard from several pastors and speakers that the Bible is "written to us." The implication was twofold: (a) God was thinking about me, a 21st Century Gentile, from the very beginning, and (b) he *used* to work through the Jews, but after Jesus ascended into heaven, he shifted to working through Gentile Christians (like me). Gesturing toward individuals in the congregation, these pastors would say, "The Bible was written to you ... and you ... and you." The sentiment was sincere. It sounded beautiful, tender, loving, and kind. If God had indeed passed the torch to me as a Gentile Christian, I felt very honored ... and (I assumed) the Jews must have blown it.

But the more I read and studied Scripture, the less likely that seemed possible – especially when passages like Jesus' circumcision undermined the premise. If God had stopped working with Israel and shifted his momentum to Gentile Christians, wouldn't it have been better *not* to circumcise Jesus? Why not remain consistent throughout and explicitly proclaim, "I am finished with the Jewish people, and I'm casting them aside to start a new religion with Gentiles, beginning with my son"?

Another way to look at this is to wonder about everything the gospels <u>don't</u> say about Jesus' childhood, aside from Luke's mention of his separation from his parents in Jerusalem at the age of twelve. Matthew briefly mentions that Jesus' family evaded Herod's death squads by fleeing to Egypt when he was a boy … but that's it. Was there *nothing* equally or more interesting in those two decades compared to the fact that Jesus was circumcised? Did he ever perform miracles as a boy? Did he ever showcase his exceptional virtue? Did he ever practice cursing fig trees? These are the kinds of things I'm interested in hearing as a Gentile.

As an author and publisher by trade … if I were trying to write a letter to move people away from Judaism into a new religion, the last thing I'd mention is how this new religion's central figure was dutifully circumcised on the eighth day! The gospels stay silent on all the other incredible stories from Jesus' childhood … but are *vocal* about his circumcision. Of all the things Luke could have shared with his audience, this one seems unnecessary. Was Luke a poor writer? Was he simply spilling random memories or stream of consciousness on paper?

For a third, lesser reason, this passage seems counterproductive. Church tradition holds that Gentile Greeks formed a sizeable percentage of Luke's gospel audience. If history is anything to go by, a Greek audience would have disliked reading about circumcision. Culturally, ancient Greeks exalted the human body's health, symmetry, and vitality. You can see it by paying close attention to their literature, artwork, and sculptures. Have you ever noticed the world's top bodybuilding competition is called "Mr. Olympia," or that one of the top hair regeneration formulas for aging men is called "Grecian Formula"? Have you noticed how Greece venerated mythical heroes like Hercules and Adonis for their peak strength and physical perfection? This is not by accident; it is an ancient Greek cultural trait.

Before the Roman conquest, the Greek Seleucid empire overran Israel. One Jewish practice the invading Greeks abhorred and attempted to abolish was infant circumcision. You can read about it in Jewish extrabiblical works like *1 Maccabees*.[22] So, if you were Luke and you knew Greeks generally found circumcision reprehensible ... What was the merit of bringing it up?

Another way to discern the significance of mentioning Jesus' circumcision is to ask, "Where else in the Bible does the topic come up?" To answer that, we can stay within Luke's writings and move to the Book of Acts, where he revealed that Paul – the very same Paul who ranted against Gentile circumcision in Galatians, turned around and contradicted himself by circumcising Timothy![23] And why did he do this, according to Luke? "Because of the Jews in that area," the text says, *"for they all knew that his father was a Greek."*

Why can't these people keep their stories straight? If Timothy's father was a Greek, shouldn't that mean *even less* reason to circumcise him? His Greekness should make him a Gentile, but Paul circumcises him ... *to please Jews?!* This doesn't make any sense. Look at this table and ask yourself – which interpretation is more consistent with what the Scriptures say?

---

[22] 1 Maccabees 1:48

[23] Acts 16:1-3

Christian Interpretations We've Heard	Jewish Interpretation
Circumcision is a Jewish rite that has no application or relevance to Christianity	Circumcision is commanded by God upon all Jewish males, including Messianic Jews, eight days after their birth
Jesus abolished and ended the Torah. His parents' decision to circumcise him is of no value or significance; they were just obeying the rules of their day	Jesus' parents upheld and obeyed the Torah by circumcising their son as a Jew, so that he could become the Jewish Messiah
Jesus started a new religion separate from Judaism. There's nothing unique or special about his circumcision; it's just common Jewish practice	Jesus called the nation of Israel to repent and return to the God of Israel and the Torah, which included the commandment of circumcision for Jewish males
Paul argued forcefully against circumcision for Jews and Gentiles in Galatians	Paul argued forcefully against circumcision for Gentiles in Galatians
Paul circumcised Timothy (who was half-Jewish) to appease some demanding local Jews and avoid controversy, but in reality he was against circumcision	Paul circumcised Timothy because Timothy was Jewish, according to tradition, and his lack of circumcision discredited him in proclaiming Jesus as Messiah to other Jews
Luke's audience were mainly Greeks, who historically abhorred circumcision and attempted to outlaw it during the Seleucid conquest of Israel	Luke mentioned Jesus' circumcision to a primarily Jewish audience living in the regions of Greece, because Jesus is the Jewish Messiah. For Jews to accept him, they would want to know details of his circumcision

Now, for everything in the left column ... if you've spent lengthy periods in Christian churches, you may think, "All of those statements are true, or at least plausibly true." But we would describe them as "partial" or "incomplete" truths, missing key details. You would have to consult the commentaries and the writings of the sages and rabbis to fully appreciate Luke's decision to include the story. You would also need to understand circumcision in its proper context – as much more than a mere medical procedure.

That will be difficult if you're fully persuaded that God has "moved on" from Israel to focus on working with Gentiles for the last 2000 years. Why bother?

For a loose parallel, imagine yourself as a mechanic trying to repair a vehicle with a carburetor, a now-obsolete technology. In the 1990s, car manufacturers began building cars exclusively using fuel injection systems.

To repair your vehicle, you would need to find specialty parts stores and acquire the filter and components of a carburetor – assuming it was still manufactured for the car you're trying to repair.

You would need out-of-print manuals to understand how to assemble and repair carburetors.

If you had trouble, what would you do? Whereas you could usually confer with other mechanics about a fuel injection system, now you'd have to find a crusty old retiree mechanic who was in business before the 1990s to talk you through it.

In the end, if you couldn't fix the car, you might throw up your hands in frustration and say, "I'm never doing this again!"

As you can dismiss the cultural context of *The Iliad* and *The Art of War*, you can (as a mechanic) get away with telling customers, "I only work on fuel injection vehicles." Choosing the finer points of your occupation won't inhibit your connection with or understanding of God (unless you choose a job he deems immoral or unlawful).

But the Bible is different. Whether you care to look into it or not, it remains ancient and Jewish. If you're a Christian, you can decide to build your life around it. However, you may preclude yourself from significant degrees of understanding if you insist that everything that happened before Jesus is now irrelevant.

You can ignore the Jewish context if you wish. Just remember not to be surprised if your vehicle stalls when you try to replace a carburetor with a fuel injection system.

Back to the Original Plot

What if there is substantial evidence from Luke's literary style that Luke himself was Jewish or possibly a Gentile convert to Judaism? What if Luke possessed a profound knowledge of Jewish tradition from years of studying with Paul? How would this passage begin to look different if it came from the hand and mind of a Jewish writer, writing to Jewish believers spread across the diaspora, living in cities like Corinth, Colosse, or Thessaloniki?

If Luke intended to establish a line of continuity between the Old and New Testaments for circumcision, he would have had this Scripture in mind:

"Speak to the people of Israel, saying, If a woman conceives and bears a male child, then she shall be unclean seven days. As at the time of her menstruation, she shall be unclean. And on the eighth day the flesh of his foreskin shall be circumcised. Then she shall continue for thirty-three days in the blood of her purifying. She shall not touch anything holy, nor come into the sanctuary, until the days of her purifying are completed."[24]

If we're dealing with an exclusively Jewish set of documents, the connection between the Messiah coming in the New Testament and the authority of the Hebrew Bible needs no further discussion. It's simply Jews continuing to do what Jews have always done and still do today. If both documents are Jewish, there is no competition between these two sections. The separateness, spoken or implied, by Christian doctrine is unnecessary.

Do you see how much more straightforward this is?

"But wait," you might say. "What about Paul? What about his rants against circumcision in Galatians?"

That's an excellent question that would make sense if Luke hadn't bothered to record Paul's act of circumcising Timothy. Without written evidence that Paul circumcised anyone after he

---

[24] Leviticus 12:2-4

became an apostle, the Jews had a point when they accused him of being "a man who taught everyone, everywhere, against our law and our place."[25] Paul would have been a man who thoroughly rejected and taught against circumcision, against Judaism itself, and left writings that we can read in the present day to prove it.

But Paul *did* circumcise Timothy … whose father was a Greek. We need to dig deeper into this. It doesn't make sense to circumcise a Greek man for fear of upsetting a group of Jews.

It's important to know, if you're a Gentile that Jews could care less whether Gentiles get circumcised. They discourage Gentiles from the practice, even if Gentiles sincerely want to become Jews. Remember: to observant Jews, circumcision implies something profound. This isn't "just a ritual," like shaving your head when you join a college fraternity. To Jews, circumcision is a sign of identification and citizenship in the Jewish nation. That's why it's painful and permanent. If a Gentile goes through it in the presence of Jewish religious leaders, it means that Gentile has become a Jew. It means they receive all the privileges, as well as all the responsibilities, of being a Jew. As Paul confirmed in Galatians, "If you are circumcised, you are obligated to obey the whole Torah!"[26]

If Paul was opposed both to the circumcision of Gentiles *and* the religion of Judaism in general … Why circumcise Timothy, the son of a Gentile, to avoid offending a bunch of Jews? It is overwhelmingly contradictory; it's the dumbest thing Paul could

25 Acts 21:28

26 Galatians 5:3

have done. What a waste of time, energy, and effort, and an abundance of personal pain in a highly private part of the body, to please a bunch of people who could care less!

Did Paul circumcise all of his closest disciples? No! There's more evidence, directly from Scripture, that when Paul met with the Jerusalem Council that "not even Titus, who was with me, was compelled to be circumcised, even though he was a Greek."[27]

So now we have an instance of a devout, observant Gentile (Titus), a close apprentice of Paul,[28] appearing before the apostles in Jerusalem … and no circumcision is necessary. Why not? According to our modern understanding of nationalities, Titus is as Greek as Timothy is, but Paul leaves Titus uncircumcised, and the elders in Jerusalem don't bat an eyelid.

So Why Circumcise?

The only answer that makes sense regarding Paul's circumcision of Timothy is that Timothy was, according to Jewish law, <u>Jewish</u> – and that the believers Paul wanted to avoid offending were Jewish believers in Jesus – what we today would call "Messianic Jews."

Let's take a modern example to illustrate. Suppose the influential Messianic Jewish author and rabbi, Jonathan Cahn, ran around making media appearances, giving speeches, and selling his books while uncircumcised. Would leading Orthodox or Chasidic

---

[27] Galatians 2:1-3

[28] Titus 1:4

Jewish leaders like Rabbi Daniel Lapin or Rabbi Manis Friedman care?

No, they would not. They pay no attention to what Rabbi Cahn does. But I (Doron) do, as a fellow Messianic Jew and rabbi. If I learned he was out of compliance with the Torah, I would confront him and remind him of his obligation under it. But if a Gentile from our same shared tradition did it ... I wouldn't breathe a word.

So, let's let the evidence speak. In his second letter to Timothy, Paul referenced Timothy's mother, Eunice, by name.[29] But in Acts, Luke mentioned her only by her nationality and faith: she was "Jewish and a believer."[30] Timothy's heritage corresponds to modern Orthodox Jewish interpretations of what makes a person "ethnically" Jewish. They believe citizenship as a Jew requires:

- Birth through a Jewish mother (even if the father is not Jewish)

- Circumcision for males

Both Messianic and Orthodox Jews generally agree that this set of circumstances made Timothy a Jew. Any way you slice it, at a minimum, he was Jewish.

On the other hand, Titus was classified as a "Greek." He had no Jewish parents on either side of his family. Luke says

---

[29] 2 Timothy 1:5

[30] Acts 16:1

nothing else about his nationality or background, and nobody at the Jerusalem Council demanded his circumcision.

There was a problem for Timothy, however … he *wasn't* circumcised.

Perhaps Timothy's Greek father objected to the practice because Greeks thought of circumcision as barbaric mutilation of the flesh. (This is an example of speculation. While the gospel writers did not mention Timothy's father by name, they *did* mention his nationality. We can, therefore, deduce from prevailing Greek attitudes about human symmetry, vitality, perfection, and health – the odds are that Timothy's dad objected to circumcising his son.)

If this is true, then Paul *had* to circumcise Timothy because the (Messianic) Jews in Lystra and Iconium "all knew that his father was a Greek." They would have suspected that something was missing, especially if Timothy's father wasn't fond of Jewish practices like circumcision. They might even have known him as an acquaintance and been aware of his objections. As Jews, they would have objected to a fellow Jew leading the local Messianic community without the appropriate marks of circumcision.

This makes Paul's actions entirely consistent with what he taught and wrote: Jews should get circumcised, Gentiles should not.[31]

---

[31] 1 Corinthians 7:18

But you might wonder, "Okay, but how would those Jews in Lystra and Iconium *know* that Timothy wasn't circumcised? Did they require him to pull down his pants and prove it before they'd listen to him?"

That's a fair question, but our answer will only make sense within the traditions and ethics of Judaism. You'll be relieved (as we were) to learn it was improbable, not to mention antisocial, for Jews to verify their identity by flashing their genitalia at one another. You did not have to lift your robes and "prove it" before other Jews would listen to you.

(Even so, had such an occasion arisen, circumcision would have been a difficult "proof" to argue with! Few Gentile nations compelled a similar ritual. If Timothy's Jewishness ever *was* questioned, in other words, he could easily prove it if he bore the marks of circumcision.)

So, what was the real reason Paul circumcised Timothy? Take heart; it's a much better reason than simply proving his identity to Jews in Lystra and Iconium.

It is very likely to have come from a deep, fundamental belief among devout, observant Jews that every human being, at every moment, is *being watched* by God. Every lie, half-truth, or misrepresentation gets recorded in the annals of the divine court. Paul wanted to reconcile Timothy to his heritage and avoid upsetting fellow Jews. However, he was even more cautious about upsetting God, an ethic we will demonstrate through other writings of Paul in later chapters and books.

From what we know of Timothy's character and enthusiasm for the Kingdom, we could also assert safely that he desired to live in complete alignment with God's commands according to the Torah. In his second letter to Timothy, Paul affirmed Timothy's faith, which he inherited from his mother and grandmother.[32] This "faith" would have been Judaism, would it not? Luke documented it that way back in Acts 16.

Christian Interpretations We've Heard	Jewish Interpretation
Timothy was an early church pastor mentored by the Apostle Paul	Timothy was a Jewish disciple of Paul, who was a Jewish rabbi and Pharisee
Timothy was half Greek and half Jewish and needed to be circumcised to avoid offending local non-believing Jews	Timothy was Jewish, even though he had a Gentile father, and needed to be circumcised under the Torah
The Jews in Lystrum and Iconia were fastidious about circumcision for everyone, so Paul circumcised Timothy to avoid upsetting or offending them	The Jews in Lystrum and Iconia believed in Jesus and knew Timothy was half-Greek because of his father. If they discovered he was not circumcised, it would discredit him, so Paul circumcised him. Plus, to be Jewish and uncircumcised is a violation of Torah

---

[32] 2 Timothy 1:5

God could care less about circumcision and only went along with this to avoid an unnecessary quarrel for the sake of church unity so more people could be saved	God commands Jewish men to be circumcised, even when they accept Jesus as Messiah, and does not tolerate disobedience or deception toward others from those he calls – especially to leadership

For Timothy to carry himself in public as a Messianic Jew and a leader of the assembly without bearing the marks of circumcision would have been disobedient toward God and dishonest toward man. He could have got away with it, at least among men, if he wanted to. But according to Jewish tradition, God would have taken issue with his disobedience and deception. (Whereas, if Timothy was instead a Christian pastor, circumcision makes no sense no matter what his identity was. But it utterly undermines Paul as a biblical authority, because elsewhere he rails against the practice for Gentiles in Galatians.)

This assumes, of course, that you can accept that Jesus came to fulfill and uphold the Torah rather than abolish or do away with it.

CHAPTER TWO
The Boy Wonder:
Did Jesus Have a Bar Mitzvah?

Thinking back to my (Doron) trip to Israel, I fondly recall our time at the Wailing Wall. Contrary to what you might assume, not everything that happens at the Wailing Wall is sad or even meant to be unhappy. Some worship activities at the wall include Bar Mitzvah ceremonies, where a young boy becomes a man according to the Torah.

I saw a group of adult men gather excitedly around a boy as he read from the Torah beside the wall. You did not have to understand a word of Hebrew to feel the event's mood. We got caught up in the anticipation of the experience. Music played through the streets of the Old City, while people threw sweets into the crowd as a group of boys celebrated their Bar Mitzvahs. With a big smile on his face, one man near us gestured for us to join him in celebrating with his family at this momentous occasion. I've never forgotten those moments, and amid the experience … I couldn't help but think of Jesus' Bar Mitzvah.

Wait … did Jesus have a Bar Mitzvah?

Did his experience look like the one I just described?

Did Joseph beam with pride and joy at his "adopted" son's coming of age?

If you're not Jewish, you could probably do with some background on the rite known as *Bar Mitzvah*. First, you should not think of the modern celebratory occasion Jews have held for their sons and daughters for the last 1000 years or so. That emerged and became a formal institution during the Middle Ages, after the destruction of Jerusalem, when the Jewish people were dispersed all across the globe.

We're instead referring to a more ancient form, traceable back to Genesis when Scripture records that "Abraham made a great feast on the day that Isaac was weaned."[33]

As it often does, English fails to convey the linguistic subtlety of Biblical Hebrew. "Weaned" is a word we usually use to connote an infant's transition from breastmilk to solid food or when a toddler stops using a pacifier. While those are certainly key milestones in child development, they're hardly as monumental as a wedding or the birth of a child.

But the original Hebrew in this passage doesn't even say "weaned." To a modern, English-speaking mind, this is even more confusing. Translated literally, it says, "Abraham made a great feast on the day Isaac *became a camel.*"

Does that raise an eyebrow or two?

"Isaac became a camel"?!

What does *that* mean? Did Isaac suddenly form hooves, sprout humps in his back, and begin walking on all fours across the Sahara, stopping occasionally to spit?

---

[33] Genesis 21:8

Of course not; biblical Hebrew is replete with analogies and metaphors. For example, when Jesus says, "My sheep listen to my voice,"[34] we know he's not speaking literally about sheep. He's describing his followers … many of whom are like sheep! As in, "Easily led (and led astray), prone to wandering, getting stuck, getting lost and needing help." And correspondingly, he calls himself "The Good Shepherd."[35]

In this passage from Genesis, the Hebrew *gemal*, translated as "camel," refers to Isaac's maturity into manhood under Abraham's tutelage. Camels, as you may know, are known for their ability to travel great distances in hot, arid climates without needing water. The spiritual parallel could hardly be more explicit; Isaac, who would go on to live like a nomad in and around the land of Canaan, had matured to the point he could survive among their corrupt, idolatrous, cannibalistic, and sorcerous cultures while holding fast to the God of Israel and the Torah.

At the time of writing, I (Paul) recently took my youngest son on a trip to the northeastern United States. To build excitement, I called it his "initiation trip," marking the time of his life (age 13) when he ascends into manhood and leaves boyhood behind. He has matured in some areas and needs to grow in others. But God showed himself to be very involved in this trip, for my son and me. We had a great adventure; we also encountered several "challenges" to test whether we'd degenerate into whiny boys or stand and face them like stoic men. I played no role in planning

---

[34] John 10:27-28

[35] John 10:11

those challenges; if you believe God is in charge of outcomes, it's easy to say that God arranged them for us.

I didn't wait until my son had achieved "full" maturity to celebrate his passage or inform him of the expectations he will shoulder as a man. I went ahead and took the trip and taught him along the way. The Scriptures never say so, but it wouldn't surprise me to learn that Abraham's feast for his son was as grave as it was celebratory. Manhood rarely waits for us to be fully prepared before testing begins. Isaac's Bar Mitzvah conferred upon a 13-year-old boy the privileges and responsibilities of an adult male, ready or not.

How would Isaac have demonstrated this maturity during his Bar Mitzvah? The Scriptures do not explicitly say, but we can infer what is *likely* to have happened based on how observant Jews carry on the tradition today. There was probably some testing involved to discern Isaac's knowledge and understanding of the Torah. It's perfectly reasonable to assume that Abraham asked questions and probed the degree to which Isaac understood and embraced his father's faith.

"But wait!" you might contend. "The Torah had not yet been given! The Jews didn't know the law until Moses came along and gave it to them at Mount Sinai!"

According to our research, this is a predominant view throughout Christendom – the giving of the Torah at Mount Sinai was the first time the Jews were exposed to the terms of the Sinai Covenant. We disagree with it, and while we could turn to extrabiblical literature to make the case more plain, we're content to stick with several passages in Genesis and Exodus that make clear – the Torah has been around much longer than since Sinai. Did the ancient Hebrews know the *full* Torah the way Moses codified it? That's hard to say. But there is ample evidence they knew its fundamentals.

Passage	Torah Law
Cain and Abel brought offerings to God, but only Abel's was accepted.	Leviticus 4 – Laws Concerning Sin Offerings
God decided to flood the world because of human wickedness and violence, but Noah found favor with him.	Ten Commandments & Noachide Laws
God told Noah to bring into the ark "seven pairs of every kind of clean animal, and one pair of every kind of unclean animal."	Leviticus 11 – Laws Concerning Clean and Unclean Food
After the flood, Noah built an altar to God and sacrificed burnt offerings of clean animals.	Exodus 20:24-26
God forbade mankind from eating blood.	Leviticus 17:13-14, Acts 15:29
God forbade murder.	Ten Commandments
God forbade adultery.	Ten Commandments
Abram built an altar to God.	Exodus 20:24-26
Abram tithed on his wealth.	Deuteronomy 14:22
Abraham circumcised himself, Ishmael and every male in his household.	Leviticus 12:2-4

In pleading for Sodom, Abraham asked God, "Will you sweep away the righteous with the wicked?"	Deuteronomy 25:1
Isaac knew the sacrifice on Mt. Moriah required a lamb for a burnt offering	Leviticus 4
Abraham's servant Eliezer gave Rebekah two bracelets, each weighing ten shekels	Two tablets, Ten Commandments
Jacob built an altar to God when he met him at Bethel	Exodus 20:24-26

At the risk of repeating ourselves … there are plenty more examples besides the ones we've listed here. But all of these occasions predated the giving of the Torah at Mount Sinai.

Most Westerners, meanwhile, know little to nothing about Bar Mitzvah, apart from perhaps some sad caricatures by secular films and liberal Jewish comedians. It is a tradition of passage for boys as they enter their formative years of adolescence. To our chagrin, Western culture abandoned initiations for boys several centuries ago. But if you understand the magnitude of Bar Mitzvah, you may begin to grasp why I draw attention to Joseph's "adopted" son. According to the Encyclopaedia Judaica:

> *"Bar/bat mitzvah is a term denoting both the attainment of religious and legal maturity as well as the occasion at which status is formally assumed for boys at the age of 13 plus one day, for girls at 12 plus one day."*

Just as we tend to diminish Jesus' circumcision, so are we tempted to blow right past the occasion of his Bar Mitzvah. We never encountered anything like a Bar Mitzvah in the churches we've attended, with which to compare it. Shall we say, "It's like when I passed my test and got my driving license"?! (To their credit, some liturgical traditions still make a parallel use of the occasion in ceremonies like "Confirmation." Children recite Scriptures, church truths and stand to be tested on their memory and awareness of their faith.)

In Jesus' day, Jews believed their children had three teachers:

- Their mothers, until they were weaned;

- Their fathers, during the ages corresponding to preschool-6th grade;

- At puberty, children were "adopted by the Torah" itself.

Life in obedience to the Torah is a matter of following specific commands – "mitzvot" in Hebrew. I don't like the term "laws" because of how Western culture and many Christian churches characterize them. They make them sound like onerous, compulsory, and punitive burdens of hardship and suffering, rigorously reinforced by holier-than-thou rabbis. This is odd because if you add up the "commands" of Jesus and the apostles in the New Testament, there are over 1000 of them ... at least 400 or so more than in the Torah.

Western history is replete with overzealous Christian leaders who butchered the gospels into messages of enforced hardship and bondage. It's not as though Christianity proved itself immune to abuse from tyrants, bigots, and religious know-it-alls.

Christian churches also have plenty of rules and regulations that constrain people from doing whatever they feel like doing in the moment. Would your church punish its pastor for an adulterous affair or its treasurer if they got caught embezzling funds? Judaism and Christianity set standards and define when violations occur, and both churches and synagogues expel members who refuse to abide by them.

So when you think of "commands," you should suspend the accusation of "heavy burdens and legalism." As far as the Scriptures are concerned, that is *sometimes* the case. However, it is not a universal characteristic of Judaism or the Torah.

"Mitzvot" simply means "instructions" – God's expressed desires of how he wants his children to live. One of them is that when a Jewish boy reaches puberty, he has his Bar Mitzvah. The word "bar" means " adopted son" (*as distinct from the word "ben," which refers to one's biological son*), while the word "mitzvah" means "commandment." So when we string the thoughts together, we get "Adopted Son of the Commandment." In the same way Joseph adopted Jesus … in this passage, Jesus is adopted by the Torah itself!

Jesus' Schooling

Jesus most likely would have spent time in Nazareth at the *Bet Sefer* ("house of the book"), the equivalent of a modern primary school where Jewish boys learned the basics of Torah from local rabbis. Promising students became students of *Bet Midrash* ("house of study"), which centered on Talmudic studies for disciples who exhibited the potential to become rabbis.

I'm inclined to believe Jesus bypassed Bet Midrash. From how Luke characterizes him in the gospel, he proved his giftedness at his Bar Mitzvah by how he impressed the rabbis. We're meant to understand this when we read, "They found him in the temple, listening to the chief priests and rabbis, and asking them questions." It's like saying, "Bobby Fischer's parents found him at the chess championships, playing against Garry Kasparov." At the tender age of twelve, Jesus engaged in lengthy discussions about the Torah with Israel's ruling and supreme religious authorities. Or like telling Catholic readers, "They found him in the Vatican, across the table from the pope, with the bishops and cardinals gathered around, listening to them and asking them questions about catechism, original sin, and purgatory."

That's hardly where the average 12-year-old boy ends up, especially when discussing matters of profound theological significance! (*It's also a clue into Jesus' fluency in Hebrew, for those of you who wonder whether or not he spoke and understood the biblical tongue. If you study Hebrew's otherworldly depth and hidden meanings, you'll conclude quickly there is no way he could possess such knowledge by studying Greek translations like the Septuagint. We'll delve into that later as well.*)

Judging by their comments in the eighth chapter of John's gospel, the Jewish religious leaders in Jerusalem seemed certain that Jesus did not learn from any of their contemporaries, nor did any formal record exist of his training at recognized schools. The text says, "They were amazed, and asked, 'How did this man get such learning without having been taught?'"[36]

I agree. For Jesus to attend Bet Midrash would have required him to sit under the tutelage of a rabbi. There's nothing inherently wrong with that – it was the way for every other Jewish boy who excelled in Torah. But in Jesus' case, that would disqualify the Spirit of God as his primary teacher. We would do well to remember his reply to those same Jewish leaders: "My teaching is not my own. It comes from the one who sent me."[37]

In other words, Jesus did not go to bed one night as a child or teenager and suddenly awaken the next morning with full knowledge of Torah. He spent nearly three decades soaking in, studying, memorizing, reciting, praying, and fully immersing himself in it, under the tutelage of the Spirit of God, before he went public as a rabbi. Of course, there was no "New Testament" to study when Jesus grew up, nor was there any other text besides the Torah! The only sacred text he could possibly have studied, to the extent of wowing the ruling Sanhedrin in Jerusalem on his twelfth birthday, was the Torah.

So, if we're reading and studying Jewish documents, Jesus' appearance at the age of twelve in Jerusalem is Luke's way of

---

[36] John 7:15

[37] John 7:16

highlighting his journey through the same customary pathway to manhood prescribed for every Jewish male who grew up in an observant family. It demarcates and affirms his authenticity as a Jew and a rabbi. Luke wrote what he wrote because it was important to the audience … he wasn't inserting "filler" language to avoid wasting paper.

Lastly, elsewhere in the gospels, the Jewish people in Jesus' hometown of Nazareth and his regular haunt of Capernaum refer to him as "the son of a carpenter." This lends weight to the notion that after his parents found him in the temple, Jesus returned home to Nazareth with his family and followed his earthly father's trade until he became a rabbi. Loosely, this echoes his regal ancestor, David, who was anointed king of Israel as a teenager but remained an obscure vagabond warrior (and fugitive) for nearly two decades until his ascension to the throne.

The Significance of Jewish Education

I (Paul) always found it puzzling that the gospels skipped from Jesus' birth to his early thirties when he went public as a rabbi. It seemed odd that the only thing we needed to know about his youth was that he made a brief appearance in the temple, hung out with the Sanhedrin, got separated from his parents, and when they questioned him, he replied cryptically, "<u>Didn't you know I must be about my Father's business?</u>"

What a strange thing to say to one's parents without context!

Some translations render his words "my Father's house," which would have also been an extraordinary statement for a 12-year-old Jewish boy to make about the temple in Jerusalem. However, the earliest Greek manuscripts indicate the sentence was left unfinished. If you translate it, the sentence literally reads: "Didn't you know I must be about my Father's …?"[38] It says neither "business" nor does it say "house." This would be an obvious incomplete sentence for anyone reading the text in English, so scholars took turns filling it in. The King James Version traditionally used the word "business." Most other versions today use the word "house."

Now, let's look at the Jewish perspective on this exchange between Jesus and his parents.

As a Jew, I (Doron) notice subtleties in the gospel, particularly concerning Jesus. As Paul noted, when a Gentile reads the "my Father's business" comment, they may be fortunate enough to intuit a positive logic or be mildly impressed by his level of devotion at such a young age. While that's true, it doesn't answer the Gentile reader's obvious question: *"What am I supposed to do with this? I love God … but I don't feel any different for having read it."*

Distinct from Catholic or other Christian rites at this age, a boy's Bar Mitzvah also meant more than crossing the threshold from childhood to adulthood. He embarked on his lifelong career,

---

[38] https://hermeneutics.stackexchange.com/questions/25880/in-luke-249-should-the-greek-text-be-understood-as-my-father-s-business-or

particularly in the days of First Century and Ancient Israel. Modern Western laws concerning education and child labor did not yet exist, so most Jewish boys' education *stopped* at this age, and their working life began, typically in apprenticeship to their fathers. If, like David or Samuel, Jesus had been anointed as a priest, prophet, and king in Israel, his reply to his parents takes on a different tone and meaning. It means he'd been adopted by Torah, and now he needed to work in his Father's business!

Perhaps it would help to picture the world's greatest athletes, like basketball star Michael Jordan or ice hockey legend Wayne Gretzky, getting dragged away from their craft by their parents and sent to flip burgers or push papers instead: "Mom! Dad! You know I belong out there practicing!"

As a rabbi, I field requests from parents who want their sons to study with me. There is honor in that, but a parent's desire for a son's destiny is different than when the son possesses the prerequisites to achieve it. A young boy needs a certain personality and competency for the role, which is usually measurable by the age of 12 or 13. In Jesus' day, most Jewish boys of that age got evaluated by their local rabbi to determine if they had the right skills and temperament.

If, in the rabbi's judgment, they failed – and 99 percent of them did – would you like to know what the rabbi usually said?

"You should go and work in your father's business."

Do those words sound familiar? This is (likely) what happened to young men like Peter, James, and John, who all ended up working for their fathers as fishermen. This was a *very* common thing for a Jewish boy of Jesus' day to hear, around the age at which Jesus quoted it to his parents.

In his case, he uttered those same words after several days of deep conversation over the finer points of Torah with the Sanhedrin, the leading religious authorities in Jerusalem.[39] In this sense, Jesus' comment is (at once) assertive, a play on words, and a tad ironic. It is neither disrespectful, nor flippant, nor uttered in ignorance. Rather, it is the simple truth. Jesus effectively said, "*Eema* (Hebrew for "Mom"), this is where I'm supposed to be, just like every other Jewish boy back in Nazareth – working in my Father's business."

Christian Interpretations We've Heard	Jewish Interpretation
Jesus grew from infancy to age twelve; no other details are provided. The cause behind his astounding literacy in Torah at age 12 is not given	Jesus grew up and either attended or bypassed a local yeshiva with the rabbis in Nazareth; he was trained and taught in Torah by the Spirit of God
Jesus went to the temple with his parents and got separated from them because he was busy listening to them and asking questions. His parents had journeyed three days back toward Nazareth before they realized he wasn't with them.	Jesus went to the temple with his parents on the occasion of his Bar Mitzvah, where he was supposed to read aloud from Torah. He wowed the Sanhedrin with profound knowledge and versatility of the law, making his career choice crystal-clear

[39] Luke 2:47

Jesus replied cryptically, "Didn't you know I must be about my Father's business?" His parents are left confused and didn't understand what he meant, and Luke says that "Mary treasured these things and pondered them in her heart." It was Jesus' way of letting his parents know he had to leave their home and be in his Father's house.	Jesus replied "Didn't you know I must be about my Father's business?" to his parents because during evaluations for future service as rabbis, Jewish rabbis told most 13-year old boys to "Go and work in your father's business." It was a play-on words and 100% truthful / accurate

Call of Duty

Once the details became clear, this reminded me (Paul) of an old war story.

Unless you've served as a soldier, you might find scenes and depictions of military life in movies like *Full Metal Jacket* or *We Were Soldiers* odd. If I watch them with my family or civilian friends who never served, they enjoy the humorous side: obnoxious military leaders barking orders and insulting or degrading subordinates is amusing and entertaining. Explosions and valorous scenes of heroism usually follow, and we admire the bravery of men in uniform.

However, if I watch those same movies with fellow military veterans, the shared meaning is more profound. We laugh heartily, recalling our own experiences of being verbally abused by drill instructors.

But we also remember what it prepared us for — a season of life where we forsook ordinary civil liberties and privileges. It was a time when we could no longer come and go as we pleased, nor choose what clothing we wore, how we styled our hair, or how we spoke to people who outranked us. It was a time when the words "I have to go to work" could mean much more than a simple eight-hour day at the office; it could mean months or years away from loved ones, exposed to extreme danger, with no guarantee of return, living (and possibly dying) by the sword. We *needed* the rite of passage of basic combat training, and we fondly remember how it shaped and molded us.

If another military veteran tells me about their basic training experience, I understand it at an intimate level most civilians fail to fully appreciate. If I talk to a combat veteran who fought in Vietnam, Korea, Iraq, or Afghanistan — there's an even greater degree of "rarefied air."

I think this is generally parallel to the difference between Gentiles and Jews. A Gentile who reads that Jesus was circumcised and went through a Bar Mitzvah absorbs simple information. He attaches no significance to it because his own culture has no such traditions. (*Though certain nomadic cultures like the Kenyan Masai tribe might see the parallel. They still initiate their boys around the same age. Apparently, they also undergo circumcision.*)[40]

But a Jew who reads the same passage understands what the Gentile fails to grasp because the Gentile never wore the "uniform" of Jewry. A Jew knows the complexity and burden of

---

[40] https://maasai-association.org/ ceremonies.html#:~:text=In%20order%20for%20the%20boy,place%20 on%20the%20eighth%20day.

serving God as a Jew. They know the privileges and advantages they receive as a birthright, but also the profound responsibilities and restrictions imposed on them which Gentiles may freely disregard.

William Shakespeare once wrote a poignant, parallel line in his play *Henry V* about the burdens of kings versus ordinary citizens: "What infinite heart's-ease must kings neglect, that private men enjoy!"[41]

I think the same is true for the Jew — particularly the Messianic Jew, who believes Jesus is the promised Messiah. What infinite heart's ease they forsake, caught in a "no man's land" between the traditions of Judaism and Christianity. How awkward they must feel with both the larger tents of faith! They must obey the Torah, just like Jews; they must also cling to Jesus and rely on someone greater than the covenant of Sinai, which Christianity emphasizes.

But any Jew knows privileges and obligations, joys and sorrows, secrets and mysteries of being Jewish. Unfortunately, they go right over Gentile heads.

If this is true, and you present a lifelong observant Jew with a candidate for the Messiah, beginning with circumcision and Bar Mitzvah during his boyhood, will that Jew knowingly nod?

Probably.

---

41 Shakespeare, W., Kellogg, B., ed. (1883) Shakespeare's King Henry V. New York, Clark & Maynard.

Will that Jew assume, from the mere mention of those two milestones, that the proposed candidate grew up steeped in study, learning, and tradition of Torah?

It's reasonable to assume they would.

Will that Jew take pleasurable surprise to learn that the messiah-candidate held his own for several rounds with the most senior religious authorities in Jerusalem?

Yes. It's unusual in any strain of Judaism for a 12-year-old boy to dialogue with men like Rabbi Moses Maimonides or the Lubavitcher Rebbe and leave them marveling at his command of the Torah.

If I were a First Century Jew in Israel learning about Jesus' Bar Mitzvah for the first time, his response about "my Father's business" would make more sense. He'd received his commission and calling; now was (normally) the time to act on it. The difference was that this "Father" did not work out of a local carpenter's shop or fishing boat. Jesus belonged in the Temple, teaching the teachers! How well do you think *that* would have gone over with the Sanhedrin?

This messiah-candidate was a child prodigy, and if his parents had their wits about them, they'd have left him in Jerusalem to study with the Sanhedrin, the same way Hannah once gave up her child, the prophet Samuel, to study with the high priest.[42]

---

[42] 1 Samuel 1

In other words, if Luke's account of Jesus' Bar Mitzvah is a casual aside from a Gentile author writing to inspire and educate Gentile Greeks … it needs work.

I've never met a Gentile who considers these passages illuminating or inspiring. They regard them (as I did for many years) as biographical "filler." Perhaps, if Luke meant to capture Greek attention, he could have included stories of superhero strength or wisdom-filled allegory, like one of Aesop's fables. But few Gentile Greeks were likely to care whether he journeyed to Jerusalem at age 12 or not.

It's also safe to assume that a nondescript exchange with the Sanhedrin was unimpressive to Greeks. It would be like telling a modern-day Muslim, "When I was a boy, I once talked theology with Billy Graham." The Muslim might offer a nod and a grunt … but he certainly won't be impressed.

Absent the Jewish background and context, Jesus' response to his parents when they found him in the temple sounds cryptic, bizarre, and mundane.

But if it's the work of a Jewish author, writing to Jewish readers about critical Jewish rites for a candidate for the Jewish messiah … his story speaks volumes as soon as you read it through Jewish eyes.

CHAPTER THREE
The Teacher: Was "Discipleship" a New Fad in Israel?

Do you attend a church with a thriving, robust discipleship program in which 75% or more of the members actively participate?

If you do, may God be praised. It's exceedingly rare for churches of any size to roll out "discipleship" campaigns that receive such a high level of genuine, life-changing engagement. It's hard to pinpoint a single, overarching reason for the lackluster response. We're reluctant to point fingers or speak as though we "know" why they don't work from the safe, convenient distance of being Messianic Jewish/Gentile misfits.

But suffice it to say ... when a pastor utters the words "discipleship program," the results in most churches are painfully predictable. More than half of the congregants immediately tune it out, and the faithful minority who dutifully sign up experience less than half the results they could if the whole church mobilized.

So, what's changed? When Jesus recruited his disciples, he only needed to utter two words – "Follow me" – and several men dropped what they were doing *in seconds* and signed up to follow him, seemingly without question. They abandoned their lives, marriages, livelihoods and familiar social settings to traipse around Israel for three years with an itinerant rabbi, who regularly got into verbal altercations and physical danger with the authorities. Who drops everything they're doing for a stranger who simply says, "Follow me"?!

If Jesus could command this kind of loyalty for three consecutive years by using two words, why can't modern church leaders get their flock to show up faithfully once a week for one hour? With 2000 years of church history, shouldn't we have discipleship down to an art form? How do we go from a lifelong commitment in response to a two-word pitch ... to practically *begging* people to devote 60 minutes a week to Bible study?

It's a gross oversimplification to paint the failures of church discipleship programs with a broad brush. There's a lot of variety, from one program to the next – but if we want to understand why the words "Follow me" amount to more than a magic spell, we must return again to the time, place, speaker, and audience when we read about discipleship in the gospels.

For example, when we focus on Jesus as the teacher ... is he a Jewish rabbi or a Christian youth minister? According to the Scriptures, his disciples and contemporaries called him "rabbi," not "pastor."

It matters how you answer – because if he is the former, then the word translated "disciple" may mean something different from what you've learned. (And if he's the latter? Well ... just try walking up to a random stranger on the street and saying, "Follow me," and see what happens.)

Speaking of Jesus' disciples ... if you encounter a modern-day "disciple," how do you know? What features and characteristics come to mind? Of course, we can easily summarize it using generic words like "follower" or "student." But let's face it – many people fit those descriptions. Instagram celebrities have followers, and schoolteachers have students. What does it mean to you to be a "disciple"? Many books and programs are devoted to educating Christians on discipleship, but judging by the results … few are the disciples. These results must be disappointing for a tradition eager to see the entire world adopt Jesus as their personal lord and savior.

For a third mystery … what was it about how Jesus uttered the words "Follow me" that made them so irresistible to these men? Was there a certain intonation in his voice, or a look in his eye, or did he perhaps wave his hand like a Jedi Knight? Though the Scriptures provide sparse details, they are not completely silent.

Among the gospels, the authors include only the tiniest clues. As the brother of Simon Peter, we know that Andrew is behind recruiting Peter into the fold.[43] We also learn from John's gospel that Philip recruits Nathaniel and that Jesus makes their first encounter supernatural by describing in intimate detail where Nathaniel was when Jesus called him.[44] But for James and John, also brothers, the most that gets recorded is that they were partners with Peter, and standing nearby when Jesus called Peter.[45] As for the rest of the disciples, the authors only mention that Jesus

---

[43] John 1:41

[44] John 1:47-49

[45] Luke 5:10

selected them; it never explains who they were, where they came from, or why they complied so quickly and willingly when he called them.

So, how did they know to make such a life-changing call for a complete stranger?

The miniseries *The Chosen* did a wonderful job of tastefully filling in the gaps about how it could have happened. In the early episodes, Peter made a string of bad decisions that led him to a moment of desperation. Meanwhile, Andrew learned of Jesus' identity and tried to persuade his brother to meet him. At first, Peter was dismissive ... until the morning he expected to be arrested by the Romans for failure to pay taxes. Jesus showed up on the beach, leading to the first miraculous catch of fish. James and John, who had been out all night with Peter, stood nearby and came running to help when the boat nearly capsized under the weight of the catch. After they'd hauled in the fish, all three men were convinced. Matthew, who the Romans had recruited to spy on Peter, observed this from a distance. Mary Magdalene, James the Lesser, and Thaddeus, who'd already met Jesus by attending a Shabbat dinner with a few other misfits and outcasts, stood on the shore and watched.

If you zoom out from these scenes, you might notice a few differences from your average church discipleship program:

- The disciples all came to know Jesus primarily through word-of-mouth, personal relationships, and ordinary Jewish cultural and social life. None of them met him by turning up at official, sanctioned religious programs.

- There's little mention of "Bible study" or "discipleship." Jesus does not precondition discipleship through a religious "funnel"; instead, he goes directly to where his recruits are struggling in their real lives and performs a miracle.

- Jesus did not fling the doors open wide and try to be seeker-friendly or take his "message to the masses." Rather, he demanded immediate, lifelong commitment from a small group of hand-picked students.

- Jesus *scared people*, in a healthy way. Peter's response to the miraculous catch was to tell Jesus, "Depart from me, for I am a sinful man, O Lord."[46] Without looking down his nose at people or lording it over them, Jesus created distinctions and established his authority by the way he spoke and interacted with people. He provided the presence of a *teacher*, not merely a facilitator.

My First Discipleship Program

When I (Paul) was a much younger man, deteriorating personal circumstances led me to answer an advertisement in the *Los Angeles Recycler*. The text read:

"Santa Monica Beach apartment, free rent in exchange for assisting an exec, must be morally and ethically excellent, college a plus."

To make a long story short, I eventually became a live-in apprentice to Andrew Magliolo, a wealthy entrepreneur who lived

---

[46] Luke 5:8

with severe spinal scoliosis. He was the kind of man today's filmmakers would love to profile for a Netflix documentary series. Though weighing only 70 lbs and disfigured in several places from the neck down, Andrew became a multimillionaire through sales, public speaking, and an indomitable, determined inner spirit. He was the kind of man necessary to mentor a rudderless young man like me, preoccupied with giving my life to meaningless pursuits on the edge of skid row.

Only many years later did I understand that Andrew's presence in my life fulfilled a passage in Deuteronomy 15, where God instructs wealthy and established Israelites on how to handle an application for servitude from an impoverished fellow Israelite. During our initial phone conversations, Andrew exuded wisdom and intelligence … but never promised to educate or mentor me. He treated the entire exchange as one of mutual benefit. I needed a place to live and couldn't afford one, and he needed someone else's muscles to do physical tasks he could not do for himself. He was clear about what he wanted and believed… but did not demand that I accept or agree with him.

Andrew was highly discerning of who he accepted into his inner circle. He went out of his way to avoid interacting below the surface with most people. As George Washington would say, he was "Courteous to all, but intimate with few, and let those few be well-tried" before giving them his confidence. I landed the role of assisting Andrew mainly because I'd pre-determined to do my best to calibrate myself to how he lived. Over the next 14 months, I sat in his presence on many occasions as he talked to people on the phone or in public settings. For a man so skilled at handling people, he purposefully steered away from having a large contingent of friends. "I have very few friends," he would say. "I don't want any friends." Then he would quote President Abraham Lincoln: "If and when I die, the only friend I have is the one deep down inside of me, I will have died a happy man."

I lived rent-free with Andrew on Santa Monica Beach, one of Los Angeles' most wealthy and desirable neighborhoods, with neighbors like Keanu Reeves, Kurt Russell, and Rutger Hauer. I got one opportunity after another to observe how a successful businessman lived. He was a dynamo with people – fearless, funny, memorable, and driven toward becoming a Hollywood actor. It was a goal *anyone* would have thought impossible for someone in his physical state … but you could not discourage him. He was wise with money and fiercely protective of his time. He was a free spirit who could laugh openly at his condition. He was disciplined, thorough, and impeccably attuned to detail. He changed my life.

Andrew knew how to scare me in a good way. Though I could easily have overpowered him physically, there was no question who the "authority figure" of the relationship was. He knew many things I didn't know and how to communicate in a way that commanded a healthy sense of respect from me. I had nowhere else to go besides moving back in with my parents. I had no money, assets, connections, or prospects. I felt somewhat like Peter when he said, "What do you want from me? Anything you ask, I will do." I literally and verbally decided: "All I have to do is whatever he teaches me to do."

I am a "disciple" of Andrew Magliolo to this day; I dutifully repeat many of the good habits he taught me, especially nutrition, exercise, personal growth, and development. When I entered his service, I was an overweight, self-absorbed, habitual cigarette smoker and pornography user. When I left, I'd lost 60 pounds. I'd stopped smoking and no longer needed to look at pornography because I began to attract interest from real women.

To this day, I pay obtuse attention to the people around me in any room I enter because that's what my mentor taught me to do. I use many of his techniques for starting conversations and making myself likable and memorable to others. I pay close attention to small details and characteristics the world fails to appreciate. I think like Andrew, speak like him, and strive to achieve success similar to his.

Would you suppose a similar thing happened for Jesus' disciples, who lived on the road with him for three years? Would you consider that they probably began to dress, speak, eat, behave, and think like their rabbi? Did they become more patient, merciful, zealous, knowledgeable, rabbinic, and distinct from their fellow Israelites, or did they remain the way they were when he called them? Most Christians say, "My life changed after Jesus called me," … but how? What does that mean? How can that truly take place without the close, proximal presence of a strong leader and teacher?

Looking back on my journey, I'm confident it was a "primer" for God to send believers into my life to call me. It would not have worked – indeed, it *did not* – before I'd been through the coming-of-age year I spent with Andrew. I believe the essence of "discipleship" in First Century Israel was closer to my journey than your average once-a-week Bible study.

Don't get me wrong — studying the Bible once a week is better than not at all! But we shouldn't be surprised at the difference in results in "discipleship." It's sort of like expecting the performance of elite military black ops soldiers from your local volunteer police reservist. The local guy knows how to fire a pistol at a paper target, but that's quite different from what the Navy SEALs get up to.

Did Jesus Invent Baptism?

Through my (Doron) work in ministering to disenfranchised Christians, as well as some confident ones, I've met with plenty of controversy around the subject of baptism. Several elements, traditions, and practices traditionally considered part of mainstream Christianity come from the realm and lore of Judaism.

The rite of baptism, which Christians typically attribute to John the Baptist, is a practice Jews trace to the giving of the Torah at Mount Sinai. If you read the books of Leviticus or Deuteronomy and fail to see it, that's probably because most English and Christian translations of the Bible fail to connect the ancient act of "immersion" with baptism. They're treated as two distinct ceremonial acts belonging to two different faiths ... when in reality, they're the same.

Congratulations ... if you've been baptized, you've followed a Jewish tradition from the law of Moses.

This often comes as a shock to Christians. Some I've spoken to grew disgusted or offended to learn about baptism apart from the narrative they'd accepted. But baptism is part of the story of Israel, as far back as our time of leaving Egypt! The tradition of bathing in a *mikvah*, using living water (usually collected from rainfall), goes way back in biblical history. It is how the Jews obeyed commands from God about ritual cleanliness for worship.

To escape death, slavery, and destruction, Israel crossed several bodies of water on their journey to the Promised Land. Each crossing contained symbolic elements of "birth" and "death," with the water acting as a transitional agent. For the loosely confederated tribes of Israel, it was the process of going through a type of "birth canal." For the pursuing Egyptian army, it spelled literal death. From this tradition, Christianity draws its reference points of "putting the old man to death" and being "raised to life" during baptism. It's correct and accurate ... and it's also incomplete because it wasn't an invention of the First Century church.

When John came along, he insisted on baptism as a mark of genuine *Teshuvah,* the Hebrew word for "repentance." This is why the word most closely associated with John is "Repent!" However, for me (Paul), a question always arose when I read that Jesus showed up to be baptized. It's similar to the question John asked: "I need to be baptized by you," he said, "and you're coming to me?"[47]

---

[47] Matthew 3:14

Quite so! *Jesus* needed to renounce sin or escape from death into life? I beg to differ. Since when does he need ritual cleansing for proper worship? And why does he answer, "Let it be so for now, to fulfill all righteousness"?[48] Is he proclaiming himself "unrighteous"? I don't know any believer who would take it that way ... but *Jesus said it*, not me. So, what did he mean?

The secret, it turns out, lies in a tradition of narrowly interpreting the Hebrew word *tzedakah*, translated as "righteousness." To the ancient Greco-Roman world, as well as to the modern English-speaking one, "righteousness" connotes law-abiding, upright, moral, and ethical rectitude. It is black-and-white, right-and-wrong. To Western minds, a "righteous" person does what is right, all the time and in every situation. This is certainly one meaning of the Hebrew word *tzedakah*. It's just that it's not the *only* meaning.

In Judaism, *tzedakah* is more expansive — it also encompasses the journey of maturity and ascent toward greater responsibility and influence. Would you be surprised to learn there are "levels" of righteousness? Back in Genesis, the patriarch Judah exonerated his daughter-in-law, Tamar, by saying, "She is more righteous than I," even though both Judah and Tamar had engaged in what we regard today as acts of deceit and sexual misconduct.[49] The Hebrew word has greater room for multiple meanings than the English word "righteousness."

---

48 Matthew 3:15

49 Genesis 38:26

For thousands of years, Jews sought wisdom, maturity, and understanding through a personal development routine they derived from studying the Torah. Jews living in Eastern Europe in the 19th Century called it *Musar*. You can find the word used in the Book of Proverbs and the commentary of the Jewish sages and rabbis. Any Jew who ascended to spiritual authority in Israel possessed a good command of Musar. For Jesus to willingly submit to baptism, in other words, did not *necessarily* or *strictly* have to mean repentance from sin or escape from death to life. Perhaps this is why he said to John, "Let it be so for now, to fulfill all righteousness." There was a kind of righteousness that even Jesus needed to fufill!

In other words, "righteousness" was more than good-versus-evil or right-versus-wrong. Think for a moment: isn't it true that sometimes, the "righteous" thing to do is (technically) against the law? When Shadrach, Meshakh, and Abed-Nego disobeyed Nebuchadnezzar, they (technically) defied the ruling authorities of their day.[50] Were they righteous or not? Isn't it obvious there's more to this word, from Jesus' teachings in the Sermon on the Mount?[51] God desires inner regeneration even more than outward obedience. If you work on the former, the latter will care for itself!

Some Christians interpret Jesus' baptism as an act of "identifying" with sinful human beings. This is plausible without Jewish context. He "could" have done it to identify with sinful human beings. But if that's why he did it, it certainly doesn't fit the narrative that he came to abolish the Torah and start a new religion.

---

[50] Daniel 3:16-28

[51] Matthew 5-6

For baptism to "identify" Jesus with human beings who broke the law of Moses and invoked the wrath of God ... must therefore mean they are guilty of disobeying the law of Moses to begin with.

But God never commanded Gentiles, including the Gentiles who lived within the nation of Israel, to bathe in the mikvah as an act of ritual cleanliness or a sign of passing from death to life. It wasn't necessary because Gentiles were *never* bound to obey the Torah the way Jews were. We contend that Gentiles living in Israel were subject to seven commands, known today as the "Noachide" laws. These laws are the original seven of what later became the 10 Commandments. They're (mostly) spelled out in Genesis 9, and none say anything about ritual cleansing. The Noachide laws represented fundamental social law and order — prohibitions against murder, theft, adultery, and so on.[52]

In full disclosure, some additional commands did apply to Gentiles living among Jews in the land of Israel ... but baptism was not among them.

This means that John — himself a Levite, the miracle son of the priest, Zechariah, the same Zechariah who (according to Luke) carefully obeyed every jot and tittle of the Torah[53] — either started a brand-new tradition (a departure from Torah) or upheld the Levitical standard of baptism in a mikvah. Given everything else we've covered, which explanation seems more likely to you?

---

[52] Genesis 9

[53] Luke 1:6

Christian Interpretations We Have Heard	Jewish Interpretation
Baptism began in the First Century with John the Baptist and Jesus	Baptism began in the Torah when God commanded it for the Israelites in Leviticus
Baptismal waters indicate acceptance of and obedience to Jesus as your personal lord and savior	The journey of the Hebrews and Israelites usually involved immersion in water to indicate a transition in status, such as "from birth to death." Baptism in a mikvah became a regular Jewish observance in preparation for the arrival of God
Jesus' baptism by John somehow "fulfilled all righteousness," even though Jesus was already fully righteous, completely sinless and did not need to be "cleansed" of anything, he went ahead and did it anyway to identify with sinners and model the way for everyone else	Jesus' baptism by John (in his unique case) marked a transition to a new level of maturity and readiness for his three years of public ministry as a rabbi; the ritual aspect of baptism was perhaps secondary, or even irrelevant on that day
Jesus abolished the law, so neither Jews nor Gentiles had anything to fear if they broke it … but they somehow still needed to be pardoned and cleansed from their sin, so he submitted to and commanded baptism for both Jews and Gentiles he welcomed into his kingdom	Jesus upheld and embodied the Torah, and engaged in regular baptism in living water anytime he became (physically) ritually impure, in accordance with Moses' commandments. He commanded baptism for both Jews and Gentiles he welcomed to his kingdom

Why Did a Sinless Man Need to be Baptized by a Lesser Man?

Sadly, most of what the world understands about Judaism in the First Century gets filtered through the lenses of Christian seminaries, removed from Jesus' context by centuries and various cultural evolutions. The extended issue of John baptizing Jesus gets dragged into a narrow, shortsighted corner.

The most prevalent explanation for Jesus' baptism is that it prepared him to take on the sins of man. Upon closer inspection, you will find that this logic is not only reductionist, undermining the ministries of both Jesus and John … but also it is an inversion of the purpose of baptism in the first place. In Christian tradition you get baptized *because* of your sin, not in preparation for it. It's like taking a shower before you do outdoor work instead of afterward. John made clear in Scripture that his call for baptism led toward repentance. The traditional Christian assumption agreed: he urged people to confess sin and get baptized. But as you'll see, these two interpretations differ substantially.

In theological terms, we would call this interpretation "eisegesis." It's a form of commentary where, instead of drawing from the text, the commentator imposes an alternate meaning. In the case of baptism, seminary professors and students superimpose the Christian concept of baptism, usually in a church setting and after reciting a sinner's prayer.

On this basis, the casual church member must infer that John presented the First Century equivalent of a Christian altar call. If that's true, it also forces Jesus into a specific mold which quickly becomes problematic: Jesus was sinless, so he did not need to renounce sin nor ask for forgiveness. But to make the pieces fit, we must assume Jesus went through the process symbolically, aiming to show his plan to die for the sins of all mankind. While this idea is inspiring and heart-warming, it stems from faulty logic/theology where the Jewish context gets mishandled or dismissed. To restore context, let's look at John's baptisms *before* Jesus showed up at the Jordan River.

Immersion, in a Jewish context, is a repetitive action that prepares people for a particular religious event. It's somewhat ordinary, rather than the dimension-altering activity it's made out to be. For example, when Joshua told the Israelites, "Consecrate yourselves, for tomorrow God will do wonders among you," this is part of what he meant.[54] Joshua said, *"Take a bath, put on clean clothes, comb your hair, pray, confess your sin, and cut out the distractions."* You could loosely compare it to the hygiene you conduct before going on a first date. It's good. You don't want to leave home without it. But it's not the highlight of the evening.

This is a paradigm shift from how Christianity presents baptism as a life-changing, singular moment of earth-shattering significance for an individual believer. Particularly since, in a sense, the baptized person has usually renounced and repented of sin. Was it not enough the first time? Will the rest of the journey not also require repentance? Is there something exceptionally magical about public baptism?

We would counter that baptism should be a *regular habit* for believers, Jewish or non-Jewish. Along with baptism comes the

---

[54] Joshua 3:5

natural expectation, among Jews and Christians, that the person being baptized makes meaningful changes in their behavior. But obviously, there will be more occasions to renounce sin and mature into new levels of discipleship. Why do it just once?

In any event, what John preached *along with* baptism was the true groundbreaking news.

Season's Greetings

What event did John prepare people for? The text gives hints, albeit using clues only Jewish eyes are trained to spot — again, for the simple reason that Gentiles do not study or observe the same calendar Jews do. But if you pay attention to the Hebrew calendar, you'll notice that every year, usually in late summertime, observant Jews go through a season called "Teshuvah." Do you remember that word? It translates to the English "repentance."

Every year, for the 40 days leading up to the high holy day of Yom Teruah, translated as "The Day of Trumpets" and also known as "Rosh HaShanah," Jews observe 40 days of confession, repentance, and renunciation of destructive habits and behaviors. So for John to dwell in the wilderness and bellow "Repent!" ... right before the season of repentance adds context to an otherwise random appearance. Think of when Thanksgiving and Black Friday pass in the US: Christmas music begins to play everywhere, decorations go up, retail business soars ... and you know what's around the corner.

I (Paul) never noticed this in 18 years of studying the Bible. When I first learned it, I was skeptical; how could we possibly know that John began crying out for repentance and baptizing people right before the season of Teshuvah when the text never says so? It doesn't even mention a "season of repentance," nor had I ever heard of such a thing in any church I'd attended. The first time I ever heard it was studying with Doron.

Beforehand, if you had told me that this passage contained references to the season of Teshuvah, it would have gone right over my head. The text reveals it indirectly when Jesus shows up and receives his baptism from John. It says that he went off into the wilderness, <u>for 40 days</u> to be tempted by the evil one.[55] During those 40 days, he neither ate bread nor drank water and lived among the wild animals. When the accuser eventually left him, angels came and ministered to him.

Okay, now we've got an echo. Forty days of Teshuvah … and Jesus went into the wilderness for 40 days. So far, so good. But what's with God's strange preoccupation with the number 40? This is like his fascination with the numbers one, three, seven, ten, twelve, and so forth. He seems to pick specific numbers randomly, either to declare that he likes them or that they're "code" for detecting when he's at work. So, are there other 40-day occasions or increments in the Bible?

There are. Moses was "40 days and 40 nights" on the mountaintop with God when he neither ate bread nor drank water. He received the Torah and the 10 Commandments for the second

---

[55] Luke 4:1

time during that summit, which he then brought down to the Israelites.[56]

Moses also led them as they wandered in circles in the desert for 40 years prior to their arrival in the Promised Land. God seems to equate a season of repentance with a nice, round, big 4-0. Sometimes, it's 40 days, and sometimes, it's 40 years. Moses also left Egypt at age 40, and went to liberate his people from them 40 years later ... and then died 40 years after that.

The prophet Jonah, meanwhile, went to the great pagan city of Nineveh and proclaimed to them, "Yet forty days and Nineveh will be overthrown." Would you like to guess which 40 days he was talking about?[57] (Bonus points if you can guess why the Ninevites listened to him!) Kings David and Solomon both reigned 40 years in Israel ... get the picture?

Knowing how Judaism emphasizes personal growth and development alongside obedience and ritual purity, we should ask ourselves: "Which is more likely to lead a person away from sin? A two-second dunk, once and for all, in a Sunday baptismal? Or 40 consecutive days of confession, fasting, prayer, and commitment to maturing as a believer?"

I do not discredit or regard my baptism (or anyone else's) as meaningless, nor would I do so to any fellow believer. But if it takes several weeks to permanently change from a bad habit or behavior into a good one ... shouldn't we at least do both?

---

[56] Exodus 24:18

[57] Jonah 3:4

Shouldn't we do baptism *and* repentance? If by baptizing, we follow a Jewish ritual ... What's the harm in doing it more than once? It's not as though we're cleansed permanently on our first time. My journey through battling idolatry and deeply ingrained godless thoughts long *after* my baptism is living proof that it takes a few swings. But my morning prayers in a mikvah (in my case, my backyard swimming pool) do wonders in keeping them far from me.

Another key to placing Jesus' journey on the Hebrew calendar comes from what he did when he returned to civilization. According to Luke, the next story is that he returned to Galilee, specifically to his hometown of Nazareth, where he was invited on the Sabbath to read the appointed text. On that day, the text was from Isaiah and contains the famous passage, "The Spirit of the LORD is upon me because he has anointed me to proclaim good news to the poor. He has sent me to proclaim freedom for the prisoners and recovery of sight to the blind, to set the oppressed free, and to proclaim the year of the LORD's favor."[58]

Now, why is this important? Unlike Christianity, Judaism reads the Torah on an annual schedule known as "Parshat" or "portions." This order remains the same today as it was 2000 years ago. So, if you know when that passage is scheduled to be read in synagogue, you can tell what day Jesus read it. The portion he read from Isaiah gets read by Jews to this day on the highest holy day, Yom Kippur – the Day of Atonement. Yom Kippur falls ten days after Rosh HaShanah, which begins at sunset on Day 40 of Teshuvah.

---

[58] Luke 4:16-20

Moreover, look at the similarities between Jewish tradition on Yom Kippur versus what happened to Jesus when he read these words on Yom Kippur.

The tradition the Levites preserved for thousands of years was decreed by God himself in his instructions to the Israelites in Leviticus. The Jews were commanded to select two goats, one of which would be pardoned and the other which would take on itself the sins of the nation. The Bible politely decreed the fate of the second goat by saying, "Send the goat away into the wilderness in the care of someone appointed to the task. The goat will carry on itself all their sins to a remote place, and the man shall 'release it' in the wilderness."[59] But in practice, the man eventually "released" the goat off the precipice of a cliff, falling to its death, as a symbol of putting away the sins of the Israelites.

And what happened to Jesus, the recently returned "goat" who had been in the wilderness? Almost the same thing! Luke's gospel says that after Jesus read the scroll and declared himself its fulfillment, the people of Nazareth became enraged, drove him out of the synagogue, and took him to the precipice of the cliff on which the town was built ... to throw him to his death![60] This was not some random cockfight, where Jesus felt an extra surge of testosterone and picked a fight, and the local Jews responded in kind. This was a living embodiment and fulfillment of an ancient template!

---

[59] Leviticus 16

[60] Luke 4:28-29

Moses' 40 day-stay on Sinai concluded a highly momentous event, where God personally manifested his presence, both visibly and audibly. Moses received the tablets with the Ten Commandments. But if you read closely, there were two summits; the first one ended badly, with the Israelites worshiping the golden calf and Moses smashing the tablets of the covenant. The 40 days occurred on Moses' second summit with God, and concluded with the second set of tablets. This indicates that the golden calf took place in the summertime, between Pentecost and the Day of Trumpets; therefore, the day Moses began his second ascent up Sinai would have been Day 1 of Teshuvah.

What about when the Israelites finished their 40 years of wandering in the desert? What happened? Moses handed the reins off to Joshua, and they entered the land of Canaan, which they proceeded to conquer. (*No, the Palestinians were nowhere to be found.*) They crossed the same Jordan River where John later baptized, and entered the land flowing with milk and honey, the same one God had promised decades earlier when he brought them up out of bondage in Egypt. That increment of 40 years led to the founding of the nation of Israel – the same nation from which great names like Samson, Gideon, Deborah, Samuel, David, Solomon, Elijah, Elisha, Josiah, Hezekiah, Jeremiah, Ezra, Nehemiah, and (eventually) Jesus would one day emerge.

Christian Interpretations We've Heard	Jewish Interpretation
The Israelites crossed the Red Sea on dry land, with the Egyptian army in full pursuit. The sea closed behind them, drowning the Egyptians	The Israelites' crossing of the Red Sea corresponds to the Jewish theme of baptism, with their old life buried under the water behind them
Moses was on the mountaintop with God for 40 days and 40 nights, and neither ate nor drank while he received the commandments	Moses' 40-day stay on the mountaintop with God receiving the Torah was the first recorded season of Teshuvah (repentance)
The Israelites wandered for 40 years in the desert before God brought them into the Promised Land	The Israelites' 40-year wandering in the desert represented a macro-level season of Teshuvah
John the Baptist started the Christian tradition of baptism in the wilderness of Israel	Baptism is a Jewish tradition that dates back to the giving of the Torah at Mount Sinai
Jesus got baptized by John to identify with sinners and affirm the Christian tradition	Jesus got baptized by John as an affirmation of the opening days of his public ministry; he had no need of repentance from sin
Jesus went into the desert for 40 days after getting baptized by John	Jesus' journey into the desert after his baptism indicates that he undertook his trials in the wilderness exactly on the Biblical timeline, in the season of Teshuvah
Jesus returned to civilization in power and went into the synagogue in Nazareth and got into trouble for proclaiming himself the fulfillment of Isaiah's prophecy	Jesus' return and controversial reading in Nazareth occurred on Yom Kippur, as evidenced by the passage he read and the punishment the Jews attempted to give him

In every biblical instance where the 40-day increment appears … something truly incredible happens. God shows up personally. He showed up to Moses and gave him the Torah. He showed up for Jonah and Nineveh repented. He showed up in Nazareth, and declared that salvation had finally arrived. *That* is most definitely worth a celebration!

So, what did John prepare the people for, when he immersed people in the Jordan River?

Nothing less than the coming of their God, the faithful King, the Righteous One, the Bread of Life.

He prepared them for a newly unlocked level of the Spirit of the Sovereign Lord, personally moving among them.

John ushered in a transformative moment in the Biblical timeline, one that commanded a change of mind, a change of heart and solemn dedication to long obedience in the same direction.

But obedience to what?

CHAPTER FOUR
The Lawless One: Where Does It Say That Jesus Abolished the Law?

What is the point of going to the trouble of public baptism, purely for its own sake? Is it some kind of bizarre dog-and-pony show? Neither Judaism nor Christianity offers baptism with zero expectation of a change in the behavior of the "baptizee." Do you know any Christian pastors who baptize their flock and think, "I hope they remain exactly the way they are"? Of course not.

If we agree that both Jews and Christians expect their adherents to grow and mature from baptism ... what exactly defines their growth and maturity? What is the measuring stick to determine if a person is growing or failing?

Now is the time to take apart that troublesome word John the Baptist used when he called to the Israelites of Jesus' day: "**Repent**." But remember – either John was a Levite Jew who called primarily on fellow Jews to return to the Torah ... or he was a Christian revolutionary who called them *away* from it. It's up to us to decide for ourselves which one seems more plausible.

If John was who the Bible says he was, then he was a Levite, the son of Zechariah, a Levite priest who scrupulously observed Torah, the cousin of the Jewish Messiah, who grew up as a Jew born to Jewish parents, in Jewish neighborhoods, learning from Jewish rabbis, interacting with Jewish businesses ... and when he went public, he chose a lifestyle modeled on Elijah, one of the most famous Jewish prophets in Israel's history.

When the gospels record John's words, they are distinctly Jewish messages. We do not, for instance, find him quoting the stoic philosopher Epictetus. That is wonderful wisdom, and it frequently aligns with biblical wisdom. It's very helpful, and I use it in my own life ... but it's <u>not</u> what the gospels record John talking about. He lived, breathed, taught and embodied *Judaism*.

In fact, while the Scriptures don't explicitly say so, it's entirely possible John became a member of the Essenes, a distinct subset of devout Jews who "seceded" from the standard priesthood, and opted for an ascetic lifestyle in the desert wilderness. In protest to the abuse of Torah by the ruling Sadducees during the Second Temple Era, Essenes retreated into remote, unregulated, small communes, where they practiced Judaism at a profound, mystical level.

Given his outspoken zeal (a feature very common to Levites) and dramatic eccentrism of dressing like Elijah in the wilderness, John's membership in the Essenes is highly plausible. Think of this, the next time you read the mystical language and vivid imagery of the Gospel of John (the apostle) ... because John's gospel aimed specifically at the Essenes and other Jewish mystics.

When the apostles later asked Jesus about the Jewish prophecy of Elijah's return, Jesus told them that John *was* Elijah's spirit. He was encased in a different body ... but that prophecy too had been fulfilled.[61]

---

[61] John 11:7-15

So, if all of this is true about John the Baptist – what are we to make of his call to "Repent!"?

Who Sets the Standard?

To proceed, we must understand the difference between the 21st Century English-speaking connotation of the word "repent" and the First Century Hebrew/Aramaic connotation of the word "shuv."

When I (Paul) hear the English word "repent," I think primarily of Catholic imagery – a pitiful, guilt-stricken schlub on their knees, hands clasped in prayer, peering dolefully upward to the invisible God, pleading for mercy and acknowledging sin. I also think of loud, megaphone street preachers at large-scale sporting events, bellowing "Repent, for the end is near!" as a bunch of strangers shuffle by.

More recently, I think of evangelical pastors and speakers – who use it to describe confession and renunciation of sin. All of these focus narrowly on the *legal* element of the word: right versus wrong, condemned versus justified, guilty versus pardoned, and so forth. As we covered before with the word *tzedakah*, or "righteousness," that is certainly <u>one</u> dimension of meaning. But it's unwise to translate to English from Hebrew reductively. Remember – according to English Live, there are over 170,000 words in current use in the English language.[62] Biblical Hebrew, on

---

[62] https://englishlive.ef.com/en/blog/language-lab/many-words-english-language/

the other hand, has a total of fewer than 9000.[63] That means one Hebrew word for every 18 English ones. Should we presume that every Hebrew word has only one meaning? We don't even do that for many English words!

Let's take the simple English word "bear." It can mean:

(a) A large, furry creature with razor-sharp teeth and claws, native to forests

(b) To carry a load: "A camel *bears* water and provisions on its back."

(c) To endure: "I can't *bear* the thought of losing you."

(d) To display: "He *bears* the scars of combat."

(e) To be responsible: "They *bear* responsibility for what they did."

(f) To give birth: "She nearly died in child*bearing*."

Surely speakers of a language of 170,000 words with this many possible meanings wouldn't begrudge ancient Hebrew speakers extra meanings of their own!

At the root of the Hebrew "teshuvah" is the Hebrew "shuv," which literally (and figuratively) means "to turn around, and go back in the opposite direction."

---

[63] https://www.sots.ac.uk/wiki/hebrew/

So … what direction had the Jewish people wandered away from?

This is where the assertion that Jesus came to dispense with Torah truly becomes like *Twister*, the family board game that forces people into pretzel-like stances trying to stay upright. There are only so many codes of behavior and conduct First Century Jews could abandon! If they had not abandoned the Torah, which direction had they wandered from?

Perhaps John meant for them to repent according to Roman law? Did he fear mass crucifixions because of Jewish resentment and rebellion against Rome? He did confront King Herod, who was a Roman puppet, after all, and the Jews were governed by Rome. Paul would later admonish all believers to be subject to whatever governing authorities ruled over them.[64]

But on the other hand, Romans weren't known for their piety toward the God of Israel, were they? Romans did not do baptisms or circumcisions, nor did they observe the Sabbath, nor did they respect the temple. They were brutal, authoritarian pagans who ate unclean foods, worshiped idols and led very unbiblical sexual lifestyles. They ruled by brutal, repressive force, greed through taxation and an abysmal record of random cruelties that would make the Nazis uncomfortable.

If John called Jews to repent and return to obeying Roman law, it's strange that he also attacked Herod for adultery. Sexual deviancy, particularly among authority figures, was *de rigueur* for

---

64 Romans 13:1

Romans. It was not an offense against society ... it was completely legal for wealthy, powerful Romans to have sexual relations with anyone they chose![65] So John's decision to rail against Herod's adultery would have fallen flat, according to Roman law. To Rome, Herod's behavior was perfectly legal and acceptable. Of course, Herod was no Roman; he was an Edomite, or (as the Romans called it) an "Idumean." But if John wanted Herod to repent and return to obeying Roman law ... he was going to need a better offense than Herod sleeping with his sister-in-law.

Only two legal codes figure prominently in the gospels – Jewish law, and Roman law. Jewish law was John's preferred matrix of morality.

Now, to be fair, among the crowds of Jews who went out to hear John preach, there were probably some people who needed to hear his message from a legal angle, to escape the impending judgment of God. The God of Israel is a God of justice, he remembers what we say and do, and he will hold us accountable for every careless, thoughtless, unkind or malicious thing we think, say or do. People living in violation of the Torah need to be warned, if their lives are out of bounds according to it.

But as often as not, when Jews call each other toward repentance, they think in broader terms. As Jesus pointed out later in the Sermon on the Mount, biblical justice is not the mere absence of illegal or immoral behavior; it also includes the *presence* of righteousness. In other words, when God's people

---

[65] https://imperiumromanum.pl/en/article/perverse-sexual-practices-in-ancient-rome/#google_vignette

practice justice, they go out of their way to encourage and prod each other toward good deeds, growth and maturity. The Jews call this "Tikkun Olam," which loosely translates to "repairing the world."

Returning to the Sermon on the Mount, this is how we should read it when Jesus says, "You have heard it was said ... but I say to you." He was talking about serious crimes, like murder:

> *"You have heard that it was said to the people long ago, 'You shall not murder, and anyone who murders will be subject to judgment.' But I tell you that anyone who is angry with a brother or sister will be subject to judgment. Again, anyone who says to a brother or sister, 'Raca,' is answerable to the court. And anyone who says, 'You fool!' will be in danger of the fire of hell."*

Now think – by phrasing his statements that way, did Jesus call for legalizing the physical act of murder, and only punishing internal emotions of anger and hatred?! Of course not. He's saying, "Mere outward obedience is not enough; you can still be filled with hatred and lust, even if you don't raise a hand to your brother. I want you to be full of goodness on the inside *and* the outside." He wants us to align our hearts with our actions, and vice versa.

The Scripture That Doesn't Exist

Sometimes, when Scripture is utterly silent in any direction on a topic, it simply means the writers felt no need to address the issue.

Ancient Israelites probably shared recreational activities similar to sports and games of our day. The Bible says nothing about them, because its authority isn't necessary. Human beings are quite capable of making and enforcing rules in a sports contest by themselves; God is content to sit in the stands and watch.

Other times, if Scripture is silent, the topic is elucidated through the teachings and writings of the rabbis and the sages. Many Jews consider these works "Halacha," which means "ruling." Rabbinic texts like the Talmud and the Mishnah go into much greater detail than the Scriptures themselves for interpreting and carrying out obedience to the Torah.

For example, Orthodox and Chasidic Jews observe 39 prohibitions on the Sabbath Day. Most of these prohibitions cannot be found in the original writings of the Five Books of Moses. The rabbis felt compelled to catalog all the examples of human activities they considered "work" on the Sabbath, to obey the command to refrain from work on the Sabbath.

Now, we must remember two other important rules for studying the Bible:

If Scripture <u>does</u> speak directly on a topic, it means *the writers felt it was necessary to add it*. The books of the Bible are *intentional* writings, not random journals or streams of consciousness. If Matthew, Mark, Luke, John, Paul, Jude, Peter or the author of Hebrews wrote something down ... they believed it was important for their audience to read and understand. The same goes for all the books of the Jewish Bible.

There is <u>no</u> Scripture anywhere in the gospels that confirms Jesus abolished the law or the Torah. Both of us have read all four gospels repeatedly, in English and Hebrew, for 20 or more years of our lives.

That passage does not exist.

But in Matthew's gospel, Jesus makes a poignant statement, which Matthew felt was essential to include:

> *"Do not think that I have come to abolish the law and the prophets; I have not come to abolish them, but to fulfill them. For truly I tell you, until heaven and earth disappear, not the smallest letter, not the least stroke of a pen, will by any means disappear from the law until everything is accomplished. Therefore anyone who sets aside one of the least of these commands and teaches others accordingly will be called least in the kingdom of heaven, but whoever practices and teaches these commands will be called great in the kingdom of heaven."*[66]

Do you see the problem here?

Which law was Jesus talking about, which he came to fulfill rather than abolish?

The Code of Hammurabi?

The Code of Emperor Justinian (Roman law)?

---

[66] Matthew 5:17-19

Islamic Sharia law?

The Prussian Civil Code? English Common Law?

If Jesus sought to abolish (or fulfill) a parallel law, like Roman law ... he failed miserably. Roman laws lasted long after he ascended into heaven. Western civilizations still use a lot of them today. (Do you think it's an accident we use so many Latin phrases in our criminal justice system?) The Son of God is not a civil anarchist; we know this because even Christians readily attest that he kept the law perfectly during his lifetime. (*Yes, it's absurd to talk like this, but the myth Jesus abolished the Torah persists today. Some influential Christian leaders write entire sermons and books year-round to keep the fallacy going.*)

And what's with this foreboding promise that the law will disappear "only when heaven and earth disappear"? Is he planning to annihilate the entire universe? Will he destroy heaven and earth and plunge the entire universe into chaos? These are the kinds of dangerous interpretations we're left to make without filtering Jesus' words through the context, culture, and setting in which he spoke.

Here's the second rule: ***Scripture does not contradict itself, ever***. Not even when it "appears" to contradict itself (and we readily concede, it appears to!). Remember the lesson about Timothy's circumcision? What are we to make of that? Was Paul against circumcision, or in favor of it? Was he a doublespeak politician – voting for circumcision before he voted against it? If so, we're in worse shape than any of us know.

But if Paul was a First Century Jewish rabbi and Pharisee, a Jewish scholar of the first order ... Then we must engage in what I (Doron) call "The Idiot Test."

The Idiot Test

The Idiot Test is the most useful tool you can carry, when studying Scripture. It's where we assume two conditions before reading, studying or interpreting *anything*:

(a) Scripture is correct and reconciled to itself, and

(b) We do not yet fully understand it

That makes us, in a very loving and affectionate sense, a group of idiots. Some are more idiotic than others, but take heart! No matter how much you learn, there's always more idiocy to come. For one thing is certain: while the *gospels* do not contain statements from Jesus that he was abolishing the Torah ... the writings of Paul most certainly seem to!

Are there passages and writings of Paul that appear to contradict Jesus' statement about abolishing the law? Absolutely ... if you only read them in English, using a modern context. Here are a few examples:

- "Christ redeemed us from the curse of the law by becoming a curse for us."[67]

---

[67] Galatians 2:13

- "For sin shall not rule over you because you are not under the law, but under grace."[68]

- "I do not set aside God's grace, because if righteousness could come through the law, then Christ died for nothing."[69]

Okay. So far, the traditional Christian narrative holds up, when we exclude context.

But ... did Paul (or any other apostle, like James) write anything that both contradicted AND affirmed Jesus' words?

The answer remains the same: "Absolutely ... if you read it in English, using a modern context."

- "We who are Jews by birth and not sinful Gentiles know that a person is not justified by the works of the law, but by faith in Jesus Christ. So we, too, have put our faith in Christ Jesus that we may be justified by faith in Christ and not by the works of the law, because by the works of the law no one will be justified."[70]

- "The law is not based on faith; on the contrary, it says, 'The person who does these things will live by them.'"[71]

---

68 Romans 6:14

69 Galatians 2:21

70 Galatians 2:15-16

71 Galatians 3:12

- "You see that a person is considered righteous by what they do, and not by faith alone."[72]

Now Paul sounds like he's talking in circles. If he is a "Jew by birth," and not a "sinful Gentile," what do you make of that? Is he looking down his nose at Gentiles? Does he think Gentiles are a bunch of sinners, while he and his fellow Jews are angelic?

First, Paul sounds like he's classifying Jews as saints, and Gentiles as sinners.

But then he seems to turn against himself, by agreeing that keeping the Torah is not enough; no one, not even Jews, can be justified through the law.

But wait! Just seconds ago he told us how perfect he and his fellow Jews are ... and now he's telling us they're in the same straits as Gentiles.

It doesn't make any sense.

What about his statement that "the law is not based on faith"? It sounds good ... but then he quotes the law and makes a contrary statement that seems to say ... It *is* based on faith!

"The one who does these things shall live by them."

What does that mean? In English and without context, it sounds like Paul is trying to have it both ways:

---

[72] James 2:24

"Keeping the law does not require faith; it's 'do or die' ... but if you keep it, you will live." Just how dumb does Paul think we are, anyway? What sort of circular reasoning is this?!

To keep the apparent contradictions going, James chimed in, in his famous "faith without works is dead" passage, which many pastors quote.

The only problem is that James made it even more clear – we *are* considered righteous by what we do, and not by faith alone.

Now for the worst part ... did Paul write anything that *affirmed* Jesus' statement about preserving the Torah, without contradicting it?

Again, the answer is "Yes ... if you read them in English, using modern context."

- "For it is not those who hear the law who are righteous in God's sight, but it is those who *obey the law* who will be declared righteous."[73]

- "There is only one God, who will justify the circumcised by faith and the uncircumcised by that same faith. Do we, then, nullify the law by this faith? Not at all! Rather, we *uphold the law.*"[74]

---

[73] Romans 2:13

[74] Romans 3:31

- "Circumcision means nothing, and uncircumcision means nothing. *Keeping God's commands* is what counts."[75]

Now Paul sounds even more absurd and self-contradictory. His first statement sounds like it means, "You're not righteous if you hear the law, but only if you hear and obey it."

Really? What if it's been abolished?

If the law no longer applies ... it doesn't really matter whether we hear *or* obey it, does it? That's like telling an American they still need to pay taxes and obey the laws of Great Britain because their laws once required it on US soil. It's laughable; we took care of that problem over 200 years ago.

If the law no longer applies, how can we be unrighteous for failing to obey it?

And if we're to obey it ... mustn't we first hear it? How can we obey a law we've never heard?

Next, Paul says that God will justify the circumcised (Jews) and uncircumcised (non-Jews) by the same faith. But he argues that faith does not nullify the law; on the contrary, the followers of Jesus *uphold* it. This puts him in even more verbal pretzels. How do you uphold a law that's been canceled or rescinded?

Then he says the biggest contradiction of them all: "Circumcision (being Jewish) means nothing and uncircumcision

---

[75] 1 Corinthians 7:19

(being Gentile) means nothing. *Keeping God's commands is what counts.*"

Commands? What commands? Remember—Jews who read this letter knew exactly what "commands" Paul was talking about, because they used the same Bible they always had: the Jewish Bible. There was no New Testament.

This brings up another interesting question: if keeping God's commands is what "counts," why does circumcision "mean nothing"?

According to the Torah, circumcision is a *command*. How can it "count" and "not count" at the same time? If it had ceased to count, why did it suddenly matter so much again to Paul that he performed the rite on his disciple, Timothy?

Paul Contradicted Jesus' Words	Paul (and James) both Contradicted and Affirmed Jesus' Words	Paul Affirmed Jesus' Words (without contradicting them)
"Christ redeemed us from the curse of the law by becoming a curse for us."	"We who are Jews by birth and not sinful Gentiles know that a person is not justified by the works of the law, but by faith in Jesus Christ …"	"For it is not those who hear the law who are righteous in God's sight, but it is those who *obey the law* who will be declared righteous."

"For sin shall not rule over you because you are not under the law, but under grace."	"The law is not based on faith; on the contrary, it says, 'The person who does these things will live by them.'"	"Do we, then, nullify the law by this faith? Not at all! Rather, we *uphold the law.*"
"I do not set aside God's grace, because if righteousness could come through the law, then Christ died for nothing."	"You see that a person is considered righteous by what they do, and not by faith alone."	"Circumcision means nothing, and uncircumcision means nothing. Keeping God's commands is what counts."

We'll say it again – when Paul wrote these words, *there was no New Testament.* There were no churches, no potlucks, no baptismal founts, no pastors, no priests, no cardinals, no bishops, no organs, no pews, no tent revivals, no cathedrals, no fog machines and no Christian radio stations. Paul's letter would not even be canonized into Scripture for another 300 years.

Which means he either wrote about the Torah … or we take the risk of picking, choosing and fabricating the moral and ethical foundation of his teaching as we go.

Which is why Paul must have been talking about the same Torah Jesus did.

Jesus In Context

CHAPTER FIVE
The Revolutionary: Was Jesus a "Radical"?

"Jesus was a radical" became a popular 20th Century Western refrain to describe him, mainly to appeal to disillusioned "hippies" of the 1960s counterculture. Amid the turbulent march of secularism against the West's Judeo-Christian heritage, a surge of enthusiasm for Jesus erupted in the United States in the early 1970s, which became known as "The Jesus Movement." In an ironic twist, many of the teenagers and young adults who flocked to the banner of "sex, drugs and rock 'n' roll" in the Sixties burned out quickly, and turned instead back to their roots. In reaching out to contemporaries, it became fashionable among evangelicals to rebrand Jesus as a "radical" to their nonbelieving contemporaries.

It is laughable to suggest that Jesus wore beads and long hair, slept with numerous women, experimented with illicit substances or listened to rock 'n' roll music. But you could make the argument, loosely, that he was a "radical" of his time.

His presence and poise in verbal combat with certain Pharisees and Jewish leaders disrupted their carefully-established order. His casual disregard for man-made doctrines and seeming indifference to the Roman occupation baffled both the ruling authorities and the political radicals around him.

You could say that within his inner circle, Jesus recruited people from opposite ends of the spectrum. Matthew, for example, who collaborated with the Roman regime by collecting taxes, could represent the "educated, elite and entrenched establishment" … while Simon the Zealot, a member of a violent revolutionary faction, corresponds loosely to modern movements like the Proud Boys, the Weather Underground or Antifa.

While these comparisons have their merits in trying to grasp Jesus' character relative to the concept of a "radical," they are insufficient without Jewish context. It's just as easy, not to mention Scriptural, to make the counter-argument that Jesus was radically *conservative*.

Back to the Beginning

We should make a distinction here: applying the word "conservative" to Jesus does not mean he was a budget hawk who campaigned for lower taxes, strong national defense, traditional family values and limited government. Jesus is an eternal monarch, not a modern Western candidate for political office. Rather, the use of the word "conservative" here should spur us to think of him as consistent with the long line of priests, prophets and kings anointed by God to lead/restore Israel back to God and their founding principles in the Torah.

In other words, when you read what Jesus said and did, you should think of Seth, Enoch, Methuselah, Noah, Shem, Job, Abraham, Isaac, Jacob, Joseph, Judah, Moses, Aaron, Joshua, Deborah, Samuel, David, Solomon, Nathan, Zadok, Elijah, Elisha, Hezekiah, Isaiah, Josiah, Jeremiah, Daniel, Esther, Mordechai, Ezra, Nehemiah and John the Baptist.

You should notice that all of them preached, taught, urged, enforced, obeyed and proclaimed the sovereignty of the God of Israel, and the immutability of the Torah. With their fellow human beings, they pleaded, reasoned, sacrificed, refused food, resisted unlawful and immoral commands, rejected places of honor, risked their own lives and went to their own deaths to honor and preserve the Torah.

Did Jesus' life measure up to these standards? You bet it did. That's what we're meant to recognize when we read the gospel accounts of his sayings and actions. Jesus said "*Repent*, for the Kingdom of God is at hand." Never did he say "Revolt" – not even against Rome, which would have easily incited his fellow Jews.

The common Christian perspective on Jesus' radicalism also ties back to his complicated relationships with ruling religious authorities. Many modern Christian pastors are fond of saying, "Jesus reserved his harshest words for the Pharisees." The church has spent several decades demagoguing the Pharisees, without taking time to understand the context of the exchanges Jesus had with them. The truth is more complicated. When pressed by their members, sometimes Jesus sided with the Pharisees; other times, he rebuked them.

Radical Sabbath

For example, consider the dispute that arose between Jesus and some Pharisees when they noticed the disciples eating grains on the Sabbath.[76] If you know nothing about Jewish legal discussions, Jesus' response to the Pharisees makes it *sound* like he repudiated the Sabbath itself:

---

[76] Matthew 12:1-8

" 'Haven't you ever read what David and his companions did when he and his companions were hungry?' said the Master. 'He entered the house of God, and he and his companions ate the consecrated bread—which was not lawful for them to do, but only for the priests. Or haven't you read in the Law that the priests on Sabbath duty in the temple desecrate the Sabbath and yet are innocent? I tell you that something greater than the temple is here. If you had known what these words mean, 'I desire mercy, not sacrifice,' you would not have condemned the innocent. For the Son of Man is Lord of the Sabbath.' "

If we interpret this as modern Westerners, it sounds like Jesus is being cynical about the Sabbath, and tossing it aside in disgust with the Pharisees' zeal and nitpicking. "Look, guys, we all know what's really going on here. David and his buddies ate the bread. The priests eat it every Sabbath. What's wrong with us doing it too? You guys are just being cruel because you have power. You're butting into other people's business. The men are hungry! Let 'em eat! In fact … you know what? I own this joint … So guess what? No more Sabbath!"

Okay. If Jesus was a modern Westerner, that's a plausible explanation of what he said. It makes him sound like a union leader or worker's advocate, sticking up for downtrodden workers against a harsh, demanding boss.

But Jesus is no modern Westerner. Elsewhere, regarding the same Levitical system of worship, he acts like a zealous purist. When he enters the temple and finds people buying, selling, exchanging money, what does he do? He becomes a one-man wrecking crew, chasing the entire crowd out with a homemade whip, turning over the tables, setting the livestock free—and then verbally lambasting all the shocked merchants and traders by quoting Scripture: "It is written, my temple shall be a house of prayer for all nations … but you have made it into a den of thieves!"[77]

Clearly, Jesus cares about the Torah, the Sabbath and the Levitical system of worship. So, what did he *mean* when he rebuked the Pharisees? To understand, you have to understand the ranks of importance among key Jewish concepts like Sabbath, temple worship and human need. Jesus regularly employed this form of argument and rhetoric, known to Jews as *kal vachomer* – which loosely translates to "from the stronger case."

"What is the weightier matter?" Think of how a judge might dismiss a jaywalking ticket for the heavier work of a murder trial.

The Pharisees' decision to enforce the Sabbath went beyond what God prescribed in the Torah. While *Shabbat* is sacred to Jews everywhere, the story of David entering the tabernacle and eating the consecrated bread was recorded deliberately — as an example of when the Sabbath must "defer" to a greater priority: **human need**.[78] For this reason, Jewish law already contained numerous provisions and exceptions to Sabbath observance. Jewish doctors, for example, were obligated to break the Sabbath to save the life of a sick or injured person. As Jesus himself pointed

---

[77] Matthew 21:12-13

[78] 1 Samuel 21:6

out in the ensuing verses, Jews already knew that God commanded them to break the Sabbath to rescue an animal that fell into a pit.[79]

As far as Jesus was concerned, the disciples were hungry, which constituted human need. The fact that they performed "work" to feed themselves was totally permissible.

Jesus also pointed out that Levite priests, who facilitated the Sabbath synagogue services, must break the Sabbath to render the service they're commanded to perform. Remember — the Bible never contradicts itself. Our God is not a sick, twisted dictator who enjoys pitting us against ourselves, commanding us to do one thing that incurs his displeasure, so he can cancel our obedience and punish us no matter what we do. Who would want to worship such a god? The Bible permits certain activities, which would otherwise be called "work," on the Sabbath. As important as the Sabbath is, it does not outweigh the work of the temple. And the temple, great and significant though it was, never outweighed human need.

Matthew 12:11-12

Christian Interpretations We've Heard	Jewish Interpretation
Jesus got angry with some Pharisees for nitpicking the disciples when they ate grain on the Sabbath	Jesus made an exception to Sabbath law and permitted his disciples to eat grain because they were hungry
The Pharisees were mean-spirited rulers who took the law so literally that they would rather see people suffer and starve than break the Sabbath	The Pharisees failed to inquire as to the context under which Jesus allowed his disciples to eat the grain, and had forgotten / not studied the law's provisions for temple service and human need
The Pharisees enforced Sabbath law zealously, making no exceptions under any circumstances, for themselves or anyone else	The Pharisees themselves knew and could think of exceptions they took to the Sabbath law, such as rescuing animals from pits
Jesus canceled the Sabbath by saying "the Sabbath was made for man, not man for the Sabbath"	Jesus upheld the Sabbath by saying "the Sabbath was made for man, not man for the Sabbath"
Jesus abolished the Sabbath by proclaiming himself "Lord of the Sabbath"	Jesus reformed and restored the Sabbath by proclaiming himself "Lord of the Sabbath"

"Reformer" Versus "Radical"

If this is what drove his altercations with authority, Jesus sounds more like a *reformer* than a radical. There's nothing radical about putting the priorities of the Torah back in their correct order, as opposed to uprooting or dismantling the entire system.

But to be sure, there were other instances where Jesus' Jewish audience expected leniency, or national solidarity, or compliance with tradition ... and in each case, he sidestepped their attempts to pigeonhole him, or turned their statements into teachable moments.

The Pharisees who approached him concerning the lawfulness of divorce, for example, were likely disciples from the contemporary Pharisaic house of Hillel. Though Jesus' teachings often coincided with, and even appear (at times) to quote Hillel, his narrow views on grounds for divorce would have surprised Hillel's disciples. Hillel held a lenient attitude toward divorce, and recommended broader tolerance for a myriad of reasons that led to it. This clashed with the contemporary, stricter house of Shammai, who believed the only acceptable reason for divorce was marital infidelity.

Jesus sided with Shammai. "Have you not read that from the beginning, God made them male and female?" he said. "So they are no longer two, but one. Therefore, what God has joined together, let not man separate … anyone who divorces his wife, except for marital unfaithfulness, and marries another woman commits adultery."[80]

When the Pharisees approached him with the denarius and asked whether it was lawful to pay taxes to Caesar, he saw right through their hypocrisy. Both the Pharisees and Jesus knew that if he affirmed paying taxes to Caesar, the people of Israel would regard him as a Roman collaborator; if he declared it unlawful, they'd have him on record as publicly calling for defiance of Roman law. It was a clever trick that almost worked … but it failed.

---

[80] Matthew 19:4

"Bring me a denarius," Jesus said. "Whose inscription is this?"

"Caesar's," they responded.

"Then give to Caesar what is Caesar's, and give to God what belongs to God," he replied smoothly.[81]

Jesus never called for the overthrow of Rome, nor did he affirm that Roman taxation was lawful. He reminded the Jews of something they already knew: *it wasn't their money*, and they weren't living under Roman occupation by accident. God had warned them in the Torah that they would suffer consequences for their collective disobedience; the financial effects of Roman occupation were simply the latest form of correction.

On a third occasion, Jesus' mother and brothers came to see him while he was teaching, and asked to see him. He responded, "Who is my mother, and who are my brothers? Here are my mother and my brothers," he continued, pointing to his disciples. "For whoever does the will of my Father in heaven is my brother and sister and mother."[82]

Was Jesus rebuking his mother and brothers, because they refused to do the will of God? Was this his casual, callous way of casting off his biological family in favor of people he barely knew, merely because they are committed to the same cause he is? Was he upending centuries of Jewish tradition, to include the Fifth

---

[81] Mark 12:14-17

[82] Matthew 12:48-50

Commandment? Why not just tell his family members to take a seat among the crowd? "Hi Mom! Hey guys! Great to see you! Have a seat and listen, and when I'm done, we'll chat."

Instead, he seizes the moment to identify his disciples as family members. His remark is ... commonplace, for a Jewish rabbi. If you closely examine writings like the Talmud and the Sayings of the Fathers, you'll find instances where disciples came to hold their rabbis in higher esteem and affection than their own parents. They would yearn for their day the rabbi thought of and addressed them in familial terms like "son." In effect, Jesus used the occasion to affirm his disciples, bestowing upon them a title they urgently desired: "sons" and "daughters" of their rabbi, whether or not they were related by blood.

So ... was Jesus a radical? Perhaps ... but not in any sense modern Westerners would recognize.

CHAPTER SIX
The Love Boat Captain:
Was Jesus Always Kind and Gentle?

The problem with labeling Jesus one way is that it doesn't leave much leeway for him (or us, as his ambassadors) when he violates our assumptions. As soon as you try to put the Son of God in a box, he jumps out. As soon as you try to put him on one side of an issue, he immediately switches to the other. The best way to understand who God is, or what he stands for … is to let him speak for himself, as he did to Moses: "I AM WHO I AM."[83]

There are plenty of moments, Scripturally, where the God of Israel displays his virtues of love, patience, kindness, forbearance, humility, gentleness and so forth. On numerous occasions throughout the gospels, Jesus displays extraordinary compassion, empathy, respect, courtesy, honor and warmth. And God knows, we need it. The sages of Judaism proclaim that God chose the planet we call "Earth" as the seat of his kingdom because it was the "lowest" of planets – a place where darkness ruled the roost. Genesis seems to confirm this: "The earth was without form and void, and darkness hovered over the face of the deep."[84] To live a full life on this planet, human beings need plenty of light, joy, peace, redemption and love.

Jesus and his Father are keenly aware of the gritty realities of life on Earth. They know how human beings mistreat one another, and how many of us go through life despised, rejected,

---

[83] Exodus 3:14

[84] Genesis 1:2

scorned, bullied, disrespected and under-valued. They know we fail to see what they see, or know what they know … and for that, they show immense compassion and patience toward us. We cherish the patience and faithfulness God shows us.

At the same time, there is abundant textual evidence that Jesus expressed a full range of human emotions and states of mind. He experienced sadness, loneliness, melancholy, despair, single-mindedness, indifference, confidence, boldness, anger, rage, stubbornness, exhaustion, futility, frustration, isolation, rejection, humor, playfulness and sarcasm. He dealt with First Century Jewish masculine life. He braved the elements, camped on the road, and shared the indignity of living under Roman rule with his fellow Israelites. He paid taxes to an overbearing occupying force, and worked in a trade where he dealt with customers – some good, some bad. He dealt with demands, complaints, moods, accusations, slander, gossip and cultural tension. When he became a public figure and felt the weight of the entire nation, the emotions intensified.

Jesus crossed paths with unpleasant social realities, and (in some cases) showed his followers how to handle them with honor, even if he shared their disagreement or resentment. On other occasions, he erupted with zeal and openly, publicly rebuked people, regardless of who was watching or listening.

Jesus healed many, many people … but a far greater number of people he could have helped remained sick, injured, dead or dying.

Jesus fed thousands of people miraculously, using a tiny amount of food; he also left untold millions of people hungry, or starving to death.

Jesus welcomed women and children into the small "flock" he led; he also excluded them from his inner circle, keeping company only with other adult men.

Jesus interacted with Gentiles, and even performed miraculous healings for them; he also declared openly in the gospels that his mission was strictly focused on the lost sheep of Israel, and forbade the disciples from announcing the arrival of the kingdom to non-Jews.[85]

So ... was Jesus always kind and gentle? Was he always welcoming, warm and "seeker-friendly"?

The answer is ... "It depends!"

It depends on the **context**. To answer that question definitively, one way or the other, is far too generic when you measure it against the text of the New Testament.

On some occasions, the text absolutely supports the idea of a kind, gentle, loving and patient man, overflowing with compassion and love. Jesus reprimanded the disciples for blocking a group of little kids who wanted to approach him; instead he put his hands on them, prayed for them and blessed them.[86] He

---

[85] Matthew 10:5-6

[86] Matthew 19:14

confronted a gathering of well-to-do Pharisees for their attitudes toward a local prostitute, when she came and fell at his feet, washed them with her tears and wiped them with her hair. He then forgave her and publicly affirmed her as a woman who "loved well."[87]

Jesus taught his disciples against retaliation. Instead of fighting back, they were to love their enemies, pray for people who persecuted them and bless those who cursed them. He dismissed a small mob of Pharisees and self-righteous citizens for asking him to judge a woman caught in the middle of adultery, and then forgave her and let her go.[88] He prayed aloud for mercy toward the Roman soldiers who drove spikes through his flesh, nailing him to the tree.[89] He showed mercy to the man crucified next to him, who was humble enough to declare that Jesus was innocent and begged to be remembered to the Father.[90]

If those were the only accounts we had of what Jesus said, taught and did … you could make the argument that he was as sweet and tender as they come. Particularly if we're meant to read them through a Greco-Roman or Western lens, forsaking the Jewish background and context.

But what are we to make of all the *other* passages – the ones that display a gruff, sarcastic, blunt, irate, aggressive,

---

87 Luke 7:36-50

88 John 8:1-11

89 Luke 23:34

90 Luke 23:32-43

confrontational, rude, bigoted or indifferent Jesus? What are we to think when he becomes impatient, obnoxious, prosecutorial and … gasp … *condemning*? Is this the kind of man you hear about in the average Sunday sermon?

The Relief of Jewish Arguments

The news that Jesus possessed other qualities besides kindness and gentleness is only shocking if you cling to conventional Christian narrative. It's another inconvenience of cultural Western Christendom, where politeness and reservedness take priority, for the sake of "church unity" or "winning the lost." Have you encountered such an atmosphere in your church, where you can be shunned or labeled "argumentative" because you question their interpretations and teachings? It's an interesting phenomenon, because although the Bible does plead for unity among believers … that plea comes from an abundantly argumentative group of authors! Nearly every letter canonized into the New Testament comes from the hand of one of Jesus' apostles, writing to set the record straight and correct faulty (or false) doctrines and practices in the diaspora of assemblies.

In several instances, the text of the New Testament becomes highly confrontational, dismissive or contemptuous of falsehoods (and their purveyors) and inflammatory. Paul told the Galatians that if he had his way, he would castrate infiltrators who taught Gentile believers that they must become circumcised.[91] Forgive the vulgarity … but can you imagine a modern pastor

---

[91] Galatians 5:12

proclaiming, "Anyone in this congregation who teaches Gentile believers they must be circumcised should have his penis cut off"?!

Would you want to hang out in the church lobby and chat after hearing *that*?

The apostle James devoted an entire paragraph to accusing rich believers of greed, malice, contempt and idolatry.[92] Which priest or pastor among the world's most well-to-do churches wants to stand up and preach on *that* passage? Talk about a message that could negatively impact donations for the upcoming food bank drive!

While Jesus and his disciples modeled and pleaded for unity and brotherhood among believers … if you don't understand what "unity and brotherhood" means from one First Century Jewish rabbi to the next, you end up with the results we just described. Pastors and priests today sidestep entire swaths of Scripture to avoid offending congregants … while congregants who question narrow, one-dimensional interpretations of Scripture feel pressure, spoken or not, to keep their thoughts and questions to themselves.

This is <u>not</u> the Jewish way!

Jews are known the world over for questioning, arguing and demanding substantive reasons as to why they should listen to or agree with *anything*. An old Jewish joke goes, "There is one God, two Jews and at least three opinions." If you think Greek

---

[92] James 5:1-6

philosophers like Socrates are famous for their questions, wait until you delve into the Jewish traditions of argument and rhetorical questioning! Most Jews wear the label like a badge of honor; it is part and parcel of being a Jew, especially if you're a rabbi.

Let's put it another way, using the examples in the text. If Jesus and the apostles were so fond of everyone getting along, being nice and avoiding confrontation … Why do we read so many examples of them refusing to compromise, lower their standards or back away from an argument? Why did Jesus himself keep poking the bears of the Pharisees, Herod and Rome, if what he really wanted was for everyone to be nice to one another?

Why didn't Jesus back down and rebuke his disciples for eating grain on the Sabbath, in the name of unity? Why didn't he wash his hands before eating, or scold the disciples for failing to wash theirs? Why didn't Paul just go ahead and permit the circumcision of Gentiles, in the name of everyone getting along? Why didn't James suck up to rich believers, rather than confront them in his letter? Why did John write that people who claim to be without sin are "liars" who walk in darkness"?[93] These statements don't go over well at cocktail parties!

But the answer is simple – these men were all Jews, and rabbis.

To Jews, and especially rabbis – assertions, questions and arguments are opportunities to *wrestle* with the text and more fully understand it. Go to a Jewish Bible study led by a rabbi, if you

---

[93] 1 John 1:8

want proof. The format is different from what you'd expect in a Christian setting. The rabbi may lead off with a topic or portion of Scripture, but the process quickly becomes interactive as the students drill the rabbi with questions, misinterpretations, alternatives and angles. (We do this all the time in our little online yeshiva!) Jews do not cling nearly as tightly to a single, narrow interpretation of Scripture the way many Christians do. In fact, according to rabbinic tradition, the duty of all disciples is to learn the "four methods" of reading and studying the Torah:

- **Peshat** – the simple, literal reading of the text

- **Remez** – the hints and allusions of the text

- **Drush** – the deeper meaning of the text

- **Sod** – the secret, mystical meaning of the text

As you'll see, the further we dig into this, the more the sayings of Jesus and the writings of the apostles are loaded with all four of these categories. But this should suffice as proof that studying Scripture requires far more than memorization. We are *supposed* to discuss, debate, challenge, and immerse ourselves in its meaning to find God's hidden wisdom.

I (Paul) dreaded bringing up a question that had haunted me for close to a decade when I began to study with Doron. Neither of my parents were believers in Jesus, up to and including their deaths. Despite numerous prayers and several attempts at sharing Christianity with them, neither of them ever repented or became believers. Under Christian doctrine, that inevitably brings up every

Christian's favorite question to avoid: "Did the person I love go to hell?"

I was relieved to discover how different the Jewish perspective on the afterlife is from the Christian one. For indeed, the gospels take plenty of moments to contemplate the fate of people who die unredeemed ... but the *interpretation* of the Western church, heavily influenced by the Greco-Roman pantheon and its mythological lore, distorts the reality. Absent the Jewish perspective on life after death, I found myself tempted to agree with the virulent atheist, the late Christopher Hitchens. In a debate with British Prime Minister Tony Blair, Hitchens said:

> *"Once you assume a creator and a plan, it makes us objects, in a cruel experiment, whereby we are created sick and commanded to be well ... And over us, to supervise this, is installed a celestial dictatorship, a kind of divine North Korea. Greedy ... for uncritical praise from dawn until dusk and swift to punish the original sins with which it so tenderly gifted us in the very first place. However, let no one say there's no cure: salvation is offered, redemption, indeed, is promised, at the low price of the surrender of your critical faculties."*[94]

Of course, once you assume <u>no</u> creator and <u>no</u> plan ... you get North Korea! But I digress.

It always seemed uncomfortable and strange to me that Christianity condemned decent people to hell, merely because they didn't believe correct doctrine. I do not find, in the pages of the

---

[94] https://speakola.com/ideas/christopher-hitchens-munk-debate-2010

Bible, a God who condemns (or pardons) people because they achieve absolute doctrinal correctness. When King Ahab, for example, carried out public repentance for his sins, did God refuse to grant mercy because the wicked king didn't believe all the right things? Not at all. God relented (temporarily) on the judgment he ordained.[95]

Conversely ... did Jesus bless certain Pharisees for their strict observance of the Torah, or did he confront them for bitterness and baseless hatred toward fellow Jews of their time? We have no need of proving it – you can read it for yourself in the Scriptures.

So you can imagine the relief I felt when Doron answered my question by assuring me that the traditional, binary Christian afterlife has little basis in Scripture, even if it has persisted well through 1700 years of Christendom. The Hebrew lens on the afterlife is much more subject to nuance and a posture I call "comfortably unresolved." There is great humility in the sages' axiom "alma d'shikra," which means "world of illusions." None of us are remotely qualified to judge the entire life of any other human being. We are blind, ironically, by what we can see with our eyes — for what we see is almost always illusory. Jesus seemed to affirm this precept when he said things like "The first shall be last, and the last shall be first,"[96] or "Those who seek to find their lives shall lose them, while those who seek to lose their lives shall find

---

[95] 1 Kings 21:27-29

[96] Matthew 20:16

them."[97] The Kingdom of God is "upside-down," as Dallas Willard said, and very difficult for us to grasp.

Tender, Tough ... and Jewish

To their credit, many Christian authors examine the Scriptures closely enough to determine that Jesus was not a soft, passive, spineless man. Yet even then, the question circles back on itself: if he was instead a rugged, confident, authoritative man who could hold his own and command respect ... why *didn't* he overthrow the Romans? Why *didn't* he use his power? Why did he only use it on certain occasions, and not on others?

Theologically, there are two possible overarching answers to this: a Jewish answer, and a non-Jewish one. If we go the non-Jewish route, we can conjecture all sorts of reasons. But if we go the Jewish route, then "Jesus is Jewish, and that changes everything," as our friends at First Fruits of Zion like to say.

So let's look first at some non-Jewish answers.

If Jesus' Jewishness has nothing to do with his recorded mix of behavior, then it's anybody's guess as to what caused him to alternate between gentle and fierce. Perhaps he was bipolar, or moody, depending on the day? Maybe he preferred some groups of people over others? The Scriptures rarely indicate the origins of his demeanor and comportment, day to day. There's as little background given when he became irritable with the disciples for

---

[97] Matthew 16:25

failing to cast out a demon,[98] as there is when he appeared to grudgingly heal the son of a Roman official.[99] Even his kindness was random, unqualified and capricious. It leaves you to wonder whether a perfectly noble action, in obedience to his commands, will garner words of praise or a sharp rebuke.

That reminds me (Paul) of my experience growing up with a mentally ill parent. I never knew which version of my mother I'd get. But one thing I knew for sure: whatever went wrong, I had to step up and be the adult, and incur any blame or consequence if I became sullen or resentful of the task.

Forgive me, but those are *not* qualities I look for in a Messiah. In fact, I'm looking for the exact opposite: someone whose wisdom, maturity and strength far outweigh my own.

Nowhere is this capricious, irrational temperament more obvious than in Jesus' interactions with the Pharisees, whom Christians adamantly characterize as his prime enemies. He warmly received Nicodemus, instead of hectoring him as a hypocrite. He taught things Nicodemus had never heard, in all his years of scholarship.[100]

Another time, a group of Pharisees warned Jesus that he'd made it onto King Herod's naughty list. Instead of turning on the Pharisees and rebuking them for merely talking to him ... he

---

[98] Matthew 17:15-20

[99] John 4:48

[100] John 3:1-21

accepts the message and attacks Herod.[101] (*But why would the Pharisees warn him, if they were his enemies?*)

Jesus affirmed the teacher of the law who asked him about the greatest commandment. He said, "You are not far from the Kingdom of God." But if the teachers of the law were a bunch of legalistic scumbags … why did he compliment this man?[102]

If this is what it means to be "tough and tender," and Jewishness has nothing to do with it … Jesus was a man of many contradictions, and his apostles were a bunch of nincompoops for recording his words and actions with so little context.

Speaking of nincompoops, have you read where Jesus labeled his closest friend "Satan"?[103] What's with that? Just one verse earlier, Peter had earned Jesus' praise for recognizing him as the Messiah. Then Jesus predicted his own death by betrayal and injustice, and Peter reacted the way any good man would if his best friend felt threatened with such a fate: "There's no way I'm going to stand by and let this happen to you!"

Couldn't Jesus simply say, "Pete, that's very kind of you and I know you love me … but this is what God has commanded"?

Yes, of course Jesus *could* have said that …

… but that's not what he said!

---

[101] Luke 13:31-32

[102] Mark 12:28-34

[103] Matthew 16:23

He turned to Peter and said, "Get behind me, Satan!" The Son of God insulted one of his strongest, most devout followers with the dark, fallen accuser of God's people as his chosen epithet. Wouldn't "Satan" have been a better label for some of the corrupt Pharisees, or Herod, or perhaps Pontius Pilate? Couldn't Jesus have given Peter a gentle knock on the head and said "Get behind me, you big dummy!"?

Yes, of course Jesus could have said that …

… *but that's not what he said!*

What is *with* this guy, and his uncalled-for aggression toward people who love him?

What about when an unnamed, aspiring disciple approached him to say, "I will follow you, but first let me go and bury my father"?[104] Did Jesus suddenly show compassion and grace to that man? Not quite.

"Let the dead bury their own dead," he grunted. "You go and proclaim the kingdom of God."

What a rude and insensitive thing to say! Can you imagine your pastor saying that, if you wanted him to wait a few days or weeks before you took evangelism training?

What about being indifferent, bigoted and rude to complete strangers? Since when does *that* qualify as "gentle and kind"? In Mark's gospel, Jesus and his disciples encountered a Syro-

---

[104] Luke 9:59-60

Phoenician woman, whose daughter was possessed by a demon. She asked him to intervene and heal her daughter. As far as Mark was concerned, that was all the context that was fit to print.[105]

Jesus could have simply said "Yes," snapped his fingers and let it happen. We know from other examples in Scripture that Jesus did not even need to be in the same geographic region to heal or resurrect people.[106] He only needed to agree to the request, and it would happen. Were he the kind, gentle person Christians make him out to be, that's what should have happened when this woman approached him.

Instead, he ignored her. He didn't even respond.

But she persisted, and followed the men around until he turned to her and said, "I was sent only to the lost sheep of Israel."

Now, if this woman had asked for a Kabbalah lesson, or the secret to becoming wealthy … perhaps Jesus could be blunt and say, "You have to be Jewish to understand."

His answer also raises another problem: "'He's only here for Jews?!' Doesn't he care about Gentiles too?"

We already know the answer to that. It ought to tell us there's more going on here than we've been taught. If Jesus was only here for the Jewish people, everybody's in trouble.

But more importantly … Jesus sounded … *cruel*.

---

[105] Mark 7:24-30

[106] Matthew 8:8

Cold, callous and casually dismissive ... of a desperate *mother*?!

This kind, gentle, patient, sweet-hearted man, pictured with children and lambs in church imagery, would tell a mother who wants her daughter to be healed ... to take a hike because she's not Jewish?!

But the story got more interesting, because even after Jesus said this, the undeterred mother persisted in her request.

So then, Jesus said something even more cruel and bitter:

"It is not right to take the children's bread and throw it to the dogs."

Okay ... now he's comparing her to a *dog*.

To First Century Jews, the degrading term "dog" could be loosely compared with modern terms like "dunce" or "ignoramus." He wasn't calling her a low-down, dirty-minded pervert; it was an expression of contempt to describe her lack of familiarity with Judaism. But regardless, his remark was a cavalier, dismissive insult.

It was also an insult that made no sense. If Jesus was (a) always gentle and kind, and (b) concerned for both Jews and Gentiles ... What are we to make of this?

As usual, we must stop and take the Idiot Test: "What if Jesus behaved the way he did because of the time, place, culture and context in which he lived? What if he was kind and gentle to some, and abrasive and belligerent to others … because he was a Jew interacting with other Jews, and (occasionally) with Gentiles?"

Have you ever spent time around Jews? How would you expect them to behave, if you went to modern Israel? Would you expect variations in behavior, from one Jew to the next? Would some be angelic, others neutral, and some unpleasant or rude? That's what you should expect, as with any society. In New Zealand, where I (Doron) live, I get similar ratios from Kiwis. They're mostly a laid-back, friendly group of people … but probably 75 percent of the people I meet are indifferent to me, in the absence of personal acquaintance. Twenty percent will make some kind of effort at being friendly … and then there is that five percent who are gruff, unpleasant and rude.

Is it possible, then, that Jesus alternated between being angelic and confrontational because, day-to-day, he dealt with *different groups* of Jews? What if some of his interactions with Pharisees were friendly, polite, respectful and affirming? What if he had friends, or even allies, among the Pharisees … *besides* Nicodemus and Joseph of Arimathea? What if some of his interactions with the Jews sound more adversarial than they really were?

As a Jew, I must let you in on the open secret – we don't fear disagreement, the way some Christian leaders have behaved when I've raised subjects like these. Remember: we're not talking about the path to eternal salvation. We're talking about whether Pharisees were good, bad, or a mixture of both.

Have you ever questioned something your pastor taught, and showed him what the Scripture says, only to have him respond, "The Spirit will reveal it to me"? I've run into a few disagreements where answers like this conveniently sidestep inconvenient truths from the text. But I could bring the same question to a group of Jews, and nine times out of ten, it would lead to a lively discussion! Judaism welcomes disagreement; we would not be good Jews if we didn't. Some Christians have more problems with questions and doubt from its adherents than others do ... but Judaism is one big nonstop family argument!

Moreover, just because Jews argue doesn't automatically make them "enemies." Remember the example of Jesus' two contemporary leading rabbis, Hillel and Shammai? It is well-known in Jewish history that these two men and many of their disciples spent their weekdays arguing ... and then showed up at each other's homes for the Sabbath dinner, where they hosted and enjoyed each other's company! (*Yes, they probably continued arguing over dinner, but that's part of being Jewish.*) So when you find Jesus arguing with the Pharisees in the gospels, don't *automatically* assume he was filled with rage, indignation or contempt for their side of the discussion. Sometimes he was outraged and put his war face on. Other times, he argued with people on friendly terms, to persuade them of a better way of thinking. Still other times ... he didn't argue at all.

So, Jesus can publicly disagree with a Pharisee without making them an enemy. But that still doesn't solve our other two problems—how he treated his friends, and his behavior toward a desperate Gentile mother.

Let There Be Light: The Gospel Makes Sense Again

I (Paul) spent over two decades baffled by these passages. At every church I attended, the men who spoke from the pulpits insisted that Jesus was utterly at odds with the Pharisees. They hated his guts, and he had no time for them either. What else could they conclude? Their default position *rejects* Jewish commentary, which leaves them in the uncomfortable position of "filling in the blanks" left by Scripture.

No preacher I ever listened to suggested that "Satan" meant anything other than "the devil," and none of them dared to try to make sense of Jesus using the devil's name as an epithet against Peter. The best I ever heard one of them speculate was, "He wasn't talking to Peter, he was talking to Satan *through* Peter."

Perhaps ... but the text doesn't say that.

I never heard a single explanation about why he told that unnamed disciple to "let the dead bury their own dead."

At the time of writing, I've sat in evangelical and other Protestant church seats for 22 years ... and never heard a single preacher take apart and explain Jesus' interaction with the Syro-Phoenician woman. (*I once heard a military chaplain frame it as "The Mother Who Wouldn't Give Up" during a Mother's Day sermon. But he made no effort to interpret Jesus' words and focused exclusively on the woman's persistence.*)

In all my years as a Christian, it was as if those passages didn't exist, or warrant examination ... and yet from those very same preachers I heard that familiar refrain: "You have to read the *whole* Bible. It's for you."

This is not an attack on Christianity or the church. Quite the opposite. For as many of those same years, in those same churches I attended, I've encountered an *overwhelming* majority of kind, sincere, generous people who live honest, conscientious lives. I have close friends, and some family members, in most Western denominations of Christianity. In our interactions, I detect only good character, thoughtfulness and an eagerness to see all of humanity restored and living well in relationship to their Creator.

Rather, I believe most Christians wield the Word of God at a fraction of the strength or understanding they could. As a result, their decisions and actions get plagued by uncertainty, misinterpretation and ambiguity, and they leave themselves prone to shame and self-accusation when they overstep boundaries they don't understand, or don't know to exist. It happened to me many times, and as I matured into mentoring younger believers, I saw them repeat their own versions of the same mistakes.

For example, let's take the phrase "in Jesus' name," which Christians attach almost universally to any prayer they utter. In the context of spiritual warfare, I heard from Christians that the phrase "in Jesus' name" was akin to a nuclear deterrent to the kingdom of darkness. I simply needed to utter it, like a magic spell, and dark spirits would flee. So when the day came for a confrontation with my mentally ill mother, I commanded the spirit I thought to be within her to depart, "in Jesus' name."

To my shock and dismay, nothing happened. In fact, she got worse. I was humiliated, and my father, a committed atheist, did not get to see his wife cured by Jesus' name. Instead, my mother had to be hospitalized for a few months. She eventually recovered, but never changed her mind about faith. She never repented, nor did she ask forgiveness, and passed away about six years later. But for me, it was too late; I had lashed out and caused a scene, doing what every Christian told me I should do in situations like that. Word spread quickly among our extended family, and I became something of a pariah for my efforts.

God remained silent. He gave me no interpretation or correction for what had happened. All I could do was sit and ask myself accusatory questions: "Did I do it wrong? Did I get the words mixed up? Was I not strong enough in the faith?"

Worse yet ... it seemed like God didn't even care or notice. That forced me to wonder, "Did I actually have the Spirit of God within me?" I felt like the seven sons of Sceva, in the Book of Acts ... except that I escaped the confrontation with my clothes on.[107] Whatever darkness plagued my mom did not even *answer* when I confronted it, much less flee. Was it all my imagination? Had I deliberately tried to make a fairy tale come true, when I should have known it wasn't going to happen?

To me, that incident was one of the clearest markers that despite all my faithful daily reading and prayer, I was blocked from understanding, or excluded from the "cool kids" of Christianity who raised the dead, healed the sick, cast out demons

---

[107] Acts 19:11-20

and so forth. It showed me that even when I prayed for things God wanted (such as healing of a spiritually destitute woman), using the special phrase "in Jesus' name" … it still didn't work. I went through some dark years of my own for the following decade, and when I resurfaced, I determined I would never again trust blindly in shallow, face-value interpretations of Scripture.

Doron helped me process through this and reframe a few things, bringing the Jewish interpretation to bear on my original assumptions:

(a) Although the Bible is written *for* us … that does not mean it is written *to* us - especially 21st Century English-speaking Gentiles

(b) Although the apostles had pronounced spiritual gifts and abilities, that does not necessarily mean modern believers have them to the same degree or strength the apostles did

(c) Not every prayer that ends with the phrase "in Jesus' name" gets granted automatically, nor is that phrase intended as some kind of magic spell to guarantee God's hand will move

(d) The phrase "in the name of" is a rabbinic refrain used throughout Second Temple Jewish literature, such as *The Sayings of the Fathers*. It is a manner of invoking recognized spiritual authority. When a rabbi wanted to make a point, they would often cite their own teachers: "Rabbi Chananiah said, *in the name of* Rabbi Yochanan …" Jesus' reference to it in the Gospel of John was directed at a specific group of people - his apostles, whom he trained as rabbis.[108]

At last, I could think clearly about what had happened. Doron's counsel relieved me of my guilt and shame, and helped me see that I'd trusted in an anemic, and somewhat baseless, understanding of certain passages of Scripture. His counsel affirmed my suspicions, without leading me away from the Son of God ... in fact, it led me closer. I realized I did <u>not</u> bear the burden of having failed to convert my parents ... nor, it turned out, would I have been held responsible if I'd avoided the course of action I took. I acted in ignorance, against my own better judgment, with half-baked theories and raw, immature interpretations of the Bible. I'd read the Scriptures too many times as a 21st Century English-speaking Westerner, completely unfamiliar with their cultural and contextual landscape.

Which brings us back to Peter/Satan, the dead burying their own dead, and the Syro-Phoenician woman. I think you'll see how these resolve neatly, in a manner consistent with what we expect from Jesus, when we consider the <u>Jewish</u> answer.

When Jesus addressed Peter as "Satan," do you picture the prince of darkness? Do you believe that the Son of God, in an uncalled-for flash of anger, conflated one of his top apostles with the dragon of Revelation? Under a Christian definition of "Satan," you have little choice; to Christians, that name has only one meaning. For some reason, using this approach, Jesus suddenly sensed Peter had been possessed by his archenemy and rebuked

---

[108] John 16:24

him as such. The text gives no explanation for Jesus' eruption, nor does it indicate Peter's response; it simply moves on to the next story.

But for Jews, the term "haSatan" – translated to "the adversary" – has a broader meaning and implication, just like the words we translate to "repentance" and "righteousness." Its interpretation is subject to context, and its precise meaning is difficult to define in a singular sense. Is the name applied to the dark, fallen being who accuses the people of God? Yes, absolutely … in context.

But is that *all* it means?

I'm relieved to say, on Peter's behalf, that the answer is "No."

To Jews, concepts like "satan" and "satanic" get interpreted more broadly. They *can* involve fallen angels, like the "Watchers" of Genesis 6 … but other times, they refer simply to the natural resistance God built into creation. If you've ever read Stephen Pressfield's book, *The War of Art*, you'll notice Pressfield uses the generic term "resistance" to describe an invisible force that stymies people from progressing toward goals and aspirations that improve their lives. That is a very apt definition of the more conventional Jewish use of the word "satan."

Orthodox Rabbi Daniel Lapin coined the term "spiritual gravity," which fits into the idea of "satan." Lapin points out that all human beings and institutions carry a hardwired tendency to degenerate, unless we actively resist and "defy" spiritual gravity.

This human proclivity corresponds to the Second Law of Thermodynamics, more commonly known as the law of entropy. Whether entropy has conscious, intellectual energy behind it or not is beside the point; it is a daily fight, in Rabbi Lapin's words, to seek the health and improvement of your faith, family, finances, fitness and friendships. But spiritual gravity is, to Jews, "satanic"; it is *designed* to oppose you and test your mettle, every day of your life.

Is it difficult to imagine the Son of God employing a name or epithet rhetorically, to make a point? To answer that, let's ask ourselves if we would ever do such a thing.

My fellow Westerners may recognize the names of two treacherous wartime figures:

- **Benedict Arnold**, a military officer who defected to, aided and abetted the British Army during the American Revolutionary War

- **Vidkun Quisling**, a Norwegian defense secretary who collaborated with the Nazis during World War II

These names became synonymous with treason and betrayal – so much so that we will often assign their names to people who commit similar acts, even though decades or centuries have passed since they died.

Now surely, if we refer to someone as a "Benedict Arnold" or "Quisling," we don't *literally* mean the men themselves, do we? Of course not. We're describing their qualities and character, or lack thereof, using symbol or metaphor, rather than simply saying "traitor."

So, when Jesus rebuked Peter and labeled him as "Satan," could he have meant something other than the red demon with the pitchfork and the barbed tail? The answer is "Yes" … as long as we look through a Jewish lens. Remember: to Jews, "HaSatan" *can* mean "the accuser," but it can also mean concepts like "resistance" or "spiritual gravity." Context is the determining factor.

So, perhaps Peter had not suddenly been possessed by the prince of darkness. Perhaps he was simply a channel for the fear and reluctance Jesus had to overcome, to accomplish his mission.

What about "Let the dead bury their own dead"? Could there be a credible explanation for Jesus' tone and choice of words?

Yes, there could … under Jewish context.

Do you recall Joseph's final request to the Israelites, before his death in Egypt? He asked them to carry his bones with them to the Promised Land, and made them swear an oath that they would bury them there.[109]

But what did the Israelites do with his body in the meantime? It tells you, in the very last words of the entire Book of Genesis: "And after they enbalmed him, he was placed in a coffin in Egypt." Joseph didn't wait to die until the Israelites left Egypt; he'd already been dead many years by the time of the Exodus.

---

[109] Genesis 50:25-26

But he did receive two different burials.

Joseph's bones eventually made it to Shechem, where they were buried in the tract of land his father Jacob bought from the sons of Hamor.[110]

Unlike modern Western funerals, First Century Jewish death rites involved two separate ceremonies. There was an immediate burial, within 48 hours of death – like what happened to Jesus' friend Lazarus, in John's Gospel.[111] But the second burial took place as much as one year later, when surviving family members moved the bones of the deceased away from the site where the body decomposed. There is definitely biblical precedent for a "second" burial, per Jewish custom.

If this unnamed disciple in Luke referred to the *second* burial of his father, does Jesus' response begin to make more sense? He doesn't seem nearly so callous, if he objected to waiting for 12 months. Even your pastor would decline to wait *that* long for you to sign up for children's ministry.

But you might say, "Well, why didn't Luke point that out? How are we supposed to know?"

You've just proved our point. It's like the modern internet refrain #IYKYK, which stands for "If you know, you know."

---

[110] Joshua 24:32

[111] John 11:1-17

In this case, it would be #IYJYK – "If you're Jewish, you know."

But if you aren't Jewish, it goes right over your head.

Besides, did Jesus take the same callous, indifferent attitude when *Lazarus* died? How about when Jesus himself died? We know he respected and honored Jewish burials, anointings and traditions ... because he participated in them, in every sense of the word.

And what do we make of Jesus' cold, sarcastic, bigoted comments toward the Syro-Phoenician woman with the demon-possessed daughter?

We know Scripture never contradicts itself, so we can dispense with the idea Jesus suddenly flip-flopped from a winsome, silver-tongued messiah into an acerbic thug. Instead, we must ask: "Who is speaking, and to whom?" We know Jesus is the speaker, and his subject is the Syro-Phoenician woman.

Unlike the nondescript, unnamed disciple who wanted to bury his father in Luke's gospel, Mark specifically mentioned this woman's nationality. There is a reason he did so; it isn't simply because Mark had nothing better to write about or he thought it would be "cool" to mention where she was from. As with the Samaritan woman in John's gospel, we must sit up and pay attention when the apostles mention details like this.

So ... why does it matter where she's from?

"Syro-Phoenician" is a vague term to most modern Westerners. If you paid zero attention in your school history class, you may have a vague geographic idea of where this woman was from. "Syria-Phoenicia," under Greco-Roman rule, was north of Israel in modern-day Syria, Lebanon and southern Turkey. Some of its key cities were Damascus, where Paul traveled on his way to a supernatural encounter with Jesus, and Tyre-and-Sidon, which Jesus mentioned when he pronounced woes on certain cities.[112] In modern times, we would probably assume she is an Arab, but in those days, a "Syro-Phoenician" woman was usually a Canaanite.

And for Jews living in the First Century, Canaanites were bad juju (no pun intended).

To 21st Century Westerners, "Canaanites" sounds like "just another bunch of people living in the Middle East in Biblical times." While that is *technically* true, it's hardly a complete picture of what they symbolized to Jews. Whenever the Bible mentions Canaan or Canaanites, we're meant to recall the ancient hostility between the sons of Noah, specifically Shem (the progenitor of the Hebrews) and Ham. According to Jewish tradition, the land of Canaan was deeded initially to Shem, but fell into its long-contested state through the adultery of Ham with Noah's wife.

"Wait a minute," you might say. "How do we know Ham slept with his mother? Genesis doesn't say that; it only says, 'Ham saw his father's nakedness.'"[113]

---

[112] Matthew 11:21-24

[113] Genesis 9:22

That's a good question. To understand the phrase "saw his father's nakedness," the first clue is to look for where else the same phrase appears in Scripture.

Does that phrase appear elsewhere in Scripture? Yes, it does.

God forbade the Israelites from incestuous sexual unions in Leviticus by saying, for example, "You shall not lie with your mother, for she is *your father's nakedness.*"[114] It is the same wording in Hebrew.

Canaan was the son of the adulterous liaison between Ham and Noah's wife, and he incurred Noah's cursing. According to Jewish tradition, Canaan was the patriarch of the barbaric, uncivilized, nomadic tribal societies that spread across the world— including into the land of Israel, where they remained until they were overrun by Joshua and the conquering Israelites.

Canaanite culture is synonymous with every destructive behavior God prohibited in the Torah – cannibalism, bloodlust, barbarism, idol worship, eating blood, human sacrifice, pagan ritual dances, child marriage, and unrestrained sexual license. If you think of the ancient Aztecs or Mayans, the aboriginal cultures of Australia and New Zealand, or many tribal societies in Africa and the Americas – bingo, you have Canaanites. Some might be literal, physical descendants of Canaan, while others are more *spiritual* heirs of Canaanite traditions. To the Jewish mind, heritage is as much behavioral as genetic.

---

114 Leviticus 18:7

In the conquest of the Promised Land documented in Joshua 1-24, God commanded Joshua to drive the Canaanites out of the land of Israel and forbid the Israelites from imitating or indulging in Canaanite practices. If you're like me (Paul), you might stop at this point and wonder, "What practices were they? The Bible never says what they did!"

But that's not true, either. You can learn what they did by studying what God <u>forbade</u> the Israelites to do in the Torah. It contains numerous provisions against all kinds of depraved, degrading human behavior ... because *that's what Canaanites did*.[115] It's what all Gentile cultures and the Jewish people do when they drift from the Torah. The same was true for all the cultures that neighbored, invaded, and conquered Israel. Whether for Egypt, Assyria, Canaan, Babylon, Persia, Rome, or Greece – God commanded against their practices and customs because *all* of them were corrupt and went against the original commands He gave to Noah.

God doesn't pull random commands from a hat and say, "Do this because I said so." He commanded Israel not to engage in incest, human sacrifice, infanticide, cannibalism, homosexuality, and a wide assortment of bizarre, gag-inducing behaviors ... because without the Torah, human beings descend rapidly into behaving like animals – predators, bottom-feeders and scavengers. Without God's law, we become more and more like ... Canaanites!

Canaanites represent a long spiritual heritage of humans who rejected God's instructions, as given (first) through Noah.

---

[115] Leviticus 18:3

Many animals engage in incest, polygamy, killing the young, cannibalizing each other, urinating/defecating/copulating in public, eating blood, eating dead carcasses, and so forth because that's how they're programmed. God has no problem with animals doing those things, but humans are meant to be different. He does not want us to behave like vulgar, vicious, evil predators. He dislikes it when we imitate bottom-feeder scavengers. If you've ever spent time in urban slums or Third World hell-holes … you've got a picture of what life is like when Canaanites run the show, and God wants nothing to do with it.

And as Western settlers and colonizers discovered … you won't get very far trying to civilize Canaanites either. They had no appreciation for Western concepts like modesty, monogamy, private property, money, the sanctity of life, or economic cooperation through trade. They had to be *taught* them.

With all of that background, does it make more sense why Jesus labeled this Syro-Phoenician woman a "dog"?

The Syro-Phoenician (Canaanite) woman came from a culture that proudly rejected the Torah and embraced hedonism, vulgarity, predatorial behavior, and worship of false gods. Her countrymen were more likely to *worship* the demon that enslaved her daughter than cast it out. Any observant Jew would have immediately kept their distance and limited interaction with such a woman lest they fall under her influence.

Is your average observant Christian all that different when they keep their distance from witch covens and Satan worshipers? What would you say if a fortune teller, a Wiccan, or a druid approached *you*, even if what they wanted was the healing of their sick child? Wouldn't you at least have *some* hesitation?

The Jews harbored similar distrust of the Greco-Roman world. Greeks and Romans worshiped idols, indulged in sexual promiscuity and homosexuality, sanctioned the killing of the unborn, and dehumanized each other and the people of the nations they conquered through slavery and trafficking. It was common in Jesus' day for the Jewish people to refer to Rome as "Edom," another name for the ancient figure of Esau. But why? How could they prove the Romans were descendants of Esau? By the time Jesus walked the earth, the descendants of Esau had been wiped out, and the only thing that remained was the region of *Idumea* to the east and southeast of Israel.

The answer is, "They couldn't." Genetic ancestry wasn't the point; *behavioral* ancestry was what mattered to the Jews. Rome behaved with the same brutality and contempt for the Torah that Esau did. As did Herod, who was an Idumean, a self-appointed king of the Jews, and an ally of Rome. Both God himself and Jewish tradition clearly state that Esau was despised because he was a base human being who could not handle the inheritance he was slated to receive from Isaac and Rebecca.[116]

With all of this in mind, how could people from such corrupt cultures even dare to approach a Jewish rabbi for a life-affirming miracle? It's unlikely to have entered their minds ... until they were desperate, like this woman.

---

[116] Malachi 1:1-3

When Jesus insulted her with the "dog" epithet, she replied: "Yes, Lord, but even the dogs eat the scraps that fall from the children's table."

Now, stop and think: what's going on here? Is she groveling, willing to take any insult he dishes out? Is this a tongue-in-cheek attempt at self-deprecation to flatter a cruel racist in exchange for a favor?

No. It's something far better. The woman's answer showed Jesus that she was on the pathway to redemption. By saying what she said, she made clear she'd been studying and learning Torah. In more explicit terms, her answer might read: "You're not fooling me. I know who you are. I've been hanging around the local synagogue and listening to the rabbi. He told us you would come, and I know what you're here to do. You're the One who was promised to Israel, and to the world. You're going to save *all* of us, not just the Jews. So here I am, ready for my salvation."

She made light of Jesus' brusque, bigoted retort because she knew who he was. She was a "diamond in the rough" of her native culture ... which was more than could be said for several Jews Jesus encountered. Elsewhere in the Book of Acts the apostle James said, "Moses has been preached in every city from the earliest times and is read in the synagogues every Sabbath."[117] The woman's response shows she was among the Gentiles who gathered near the synagogue and listened to the rabbi in her hometown every Sabbath.

---

[117] Acts 15:21

Do you understand why Jesus suddenly flashed a grin, reversed his posture, and cooperated with her? "For that answer, you may go," he said. "Your daughter has been healed." It wasn't because she showed she was willing to take any old verbal abuse he threw at her. Instead, he playfully recognized that she stood out from her native culture and conceded his bluff to a Gentile who had drawn close to Israel.

This woman was an exceptional Canaanite! As Isaiah 56 declares, she was "the foreigner who bound herself to the LORD, to minister to him, to love the name of the LORD, and to be his servant." She was one of "all who keep the Sabbath without desecrating it, and who hold fast to my covenant–these I will bring to my holy mountain and give them joy in my house of prayer. Their burnt offerings and sacrifices will be accepted on my altar, for my house will be called a house of prayer for all nations."[118]

Most assuredly, Jesus was tough and tender. The only question we have to answer is … "Was he Jewish, and does it matter?"

---

[118] Isaiah 56:6-8

CHAPTER SEVEN
The Liberator:
Did Jesus Set Gentiles "Free" From Judaism?

One of the central governing doctrines of the three great branches of Christianity (Catholic, Protestant, and Orthodox) is called "supersessionism" or "Replacement Theology." For the last 1700 years, this position asserted (to varying degrees) that Jesus came to dismantle and do away with the Torah. Exhausted with trying to get the Jewish people to listen or cooperate in their mission to be "a light unto the nations," God gave up on Israel and passed the torch to Gentiles under the banner of Christianity. Where God once operated through Jews ... he now changes the world through cheerfully obedient Christians, who are fully united (even though they've splintered into over 1000 different denominations) and do not need all those stifling rules (even though they still observe many of them).

Once again, if you read the New Testament without regard for its context, culture, native language, and setting ... there are passages and exchanges between Jesus and the people of his day that appear to reinforce this myth. That's one reason it's persisted so well. Some Christian denominations have diluted this belief into more refined doctrines, such as "Covenant Theology" or "Dispensationalism," particularly in the wake of the Nazi Holocaust and the reestablishment of the State of Israel in 1948. But in each of those reforms, elements of supersessionism creep into the sermons and literary works of their most recognizable adherents.

Supersessionists argue and reinforce the idea (or portions thereof) in Christian churches every week: "Jesus did away with the old law and replaced Israel with the church, and now we can live in freedom!" It sounds as though all of humanity, Jew and Gentile alike, were oppressed and weighed down by a burdensome, mean-spirited Torah. Jesus confronted a cruel, nitpicking, micro-managing team of Pharisees and delivered us from their clutches. He exposed the hypocrites and put the law to death so we could all live together in liberty. He saved us from "religion," as some are fond of saying, and set us in a "relationship" with God.

But to hedge against vast, amorphous ideas of "freedom," a church leader would have to backpedal if congregants took them at their word. We can easily imagine what a priest or pastor might say if you said to them, "Jesus did away with the old law. Does that mean I can violate any of the Ten Commandments, and there won't be any consequences? May I now commit adultery, or steal from my neighbor, or kill them if I don't like them?"

The Ten Commandments are "part of the old law," are they not? They're included in the same lengthy list of commands God gave Moses on Mount Sinai. Churches certainly punish and dismiss pastors who get caught in acts of adultery, or embezzlement, and they would never attempt to protect someone wanted by police for murder! Amen, and rightly so. Christians reject most violations of the Ten Commandments, and as long as everyone recognizes and agrees with that, everything's hunky-dory. To try to square this with supersessionist doctrine, they divide the Torah into three categories of laws:

- Moral

- Civil

- Ceremonial

They proclaim Christians bound to observe the moral law (except the 4th Commandment), and disregard the rest because they've been "fulfilled" by Jesus.

Conveniently, most of the Torah's civil laws are already codified among Western societies. This makes them appear to be secular laws, which makes this discussion purely hypothetical. But in reality ... where did the civil authorities get their legal ideas from? Is it purely an accident that Western societies adopted significant portions of them from the laws and ethics of the Bible? The U.S. Congress has a statue of Moses holding the Ten Commandments inside its chamber ... is this pure coincidence? Nothing to see here, move along?! We enjoy protection against cruel and unusual punishments ... and this has nothing to do with the biblical concept of "eye for eye, tooth for tooth"?!

Similarly, as we've covered earlier ... if ceremonial laws are fulfilled, why do Christians continue to observe ceremonial Jewish laws, like baptism? Why do they eat (mostly) kosher foods, avoiding 90 percent of the foods God forbids the Jews to eat?[119] They observe God's commands against eating blood[120], against

---

[119] Leviticus 11

[120] Leviticus 17

sexual immorality[121], and many Christian traditions depend (directly or indirectly) on the Appointed Times of Leviticus 23. Standard observances like Easter, Pentecost, (in the US) Thanksgiving, and Christmas all have ties to Jewish tradition.

Christians Continue to Observe Much of the Law

Would you agree that most Christians observe many of the Torah's dietary restrictions? While Western Christians feel free to consume some foods forbidden to Jews, such as pork or shellfish … most Christians do not eat bats, insects, birds of prey, or scavenger animals, do they? The church has not interpreted "freedom" to include harvesting dogs, cats, vultures, or camels for human consumption.

But why not? Other cultures around the world feel completely free to eat these animals. Camels are a halal delicacy for Arabs and Muslims, and far Eastern nations (especially impoverished ones) feel no compunction about eating animals we domesticate as pets in the West. Some cultures regard exotic seafood like octopus as gourmet cuisine. Why don't any of these foods show up at your local church potluck?

Is Christianity famous for its rigorous enforcement of "old law" sexual mores? Let's put it this way: entire subcultures and movements cropped up throughout Christendom in response to the Sexual Revolution of the 1960s. I (Paul) got swept into Christianity, among other things, by Joshua Harris' famous book, *I Kissed Dating Goodbye*. My entry into the Kingdom coincided

---

[121] Leviticus 18

with my days as a young single man, and I found the author's reverence for marriage appealing. I followed his advice, and after 19 years of committed, joy-filled matrimony at the time of writing, it paid off wonderfully. To this day, the collective Christian church tries to straddle the tightrope between welcoming sexually unrepentant people through its doors versus preserving adherence to Biblical sexuality.

But should any of this be necessary? Didn't Jesus set us "free" from the old law?

You might counter that question by bringing up the decisions of the Jerusalem Council in Acts 15, where the apostles forbid the church from eating certain foods and engaging in sexual immorality. That's quite correct … but what standard did they apply to determine what was forbidden or "sexually immoral"?

If you guessed "the Jewish standard," you are correct.

There was only one standard in the world at the time the council gave that ruling, that took issue with unclean foods and sexual relationships outside of of monogamous, heterosexual, non-incestuous, adult-only marriage: Jewish law. As we've already covered, the Greeks, Romans, Canaanites, and Arabs had plenty of loopholes, exceptions, and accepted traditions contrary to the Jewish ideal. The apostles did not yet have access to a codified, canonized New Testament; the only religious text they could consult was the Hebrew Scriptures. Do we then believe they resorted to flipping a coin, drawing numbers out of a hat, or simply making it up?

"But," you might argue, "God never seemed to have a problem with certain Jewish men in the Bible engaging in sexual immorality! Look at all the polygamy! Jacob had four wives, David married multiple women (and fathered a child with an already-married one), and Solomon had over 700 wives! The kings of Israel kept harems!"

Okay. There do *appear* to be instances where God tolerates alternative lifestyles, especially to the untrained eye of a 21st Century Westerner reading the Bible in English through a Greco-Roman cultural lens.

But if you take that to mean the God of Israel does not have a standard for marriage, we fail to solve the problem. Even if you could prove that God had "no problem with polygamy" in the Old Testament, Jesus still spoke very clearly about a Jewish standard for marriage, as did Paul. Why teach and endorse a Jewish standard for marriage, if you don't truly have one? Either God has an issue with sexual immorality, or he doesn't.

If God doesn't care about sexual immorality, why did Jesus respond the way he did, when the Pharisees approached and asked him if divorce was lawful? Jesus' response was, "Unless she is unfaithful to your marriage, you have no business getting divorced, and if you do, you commit adultery."

Shouldn't he rather have said, "Que será, será, my Father never had a problem with David or Solomon doing it, so knock yourself out!"?

If God is relaxed on standards for marriage and sexual conduct, in other words, Jesus should have said, "Moses, Schmoses! Cut 'em loose if you want to, or marry 15 of them and make them compete for your attention. I don't care!"

But that's not what he said.

Did God maintain his standard for marriage with Jesus, only to undo it with Paul? Quite the contrary. When the believers in Corinth wrote to Paul concerning the merits of remaining celibate versus marrying, he responded, "It is good for a man to avoid touching a woman. Nevertheless, because there is so much immorality, let each man have his own wife, and each woman have her own husband."[122]

Does that sound like a simple, straightforward definition of Biblically appropriate sexual relationships to you?

What about Peter? Which of these sounds more like what Peter wrote, in his letters?

> (a) "Likewise, you wives, be submissive to your own husbands ..."[123]

or

> (b) "Likewise, you baby mamas, be submissive to your baby daddies"?

---

[122] 1 Corinthians 7:2

[123] 1 Peter 3:1-2

Peter said nothing about how girlfriends should relate to boyfriends, nor did Paul. The Bible has nothing to say about how to conduct sexual relationships over dating apps like Tinder or Bumble. It doesn't even offer guidance on how to do them through more wholesome internet sites like eHarmony. It offers guidance on one type of male-female relationship, and only one: marriage.

Did God remain silent on this because he assumed most Gentile cultures had superior codes about male-female relationships? If so, he needed to get out more. On the contrary – Jesus, the apostles, the Jews and the Bible all agree on a single, uniform standard for male-female, sexual relationships: marriage.

Monogamous, heterosexual, non-incestuous marriage. For those of you in left field and some fringe denominations, that means "one adult man to one adult woman, who are not related to one another."

Okay. Enough with the sarcasm. Can we deduce, from all this evidence, that Gentile Christians study, obey, apply, maintain and enforce Jewish sexual standards to the present day? We certainly can, if they read and implement what the apostles prescribed in the New Testament, and stop pretending that they chose those laws at random.

On the flipside, if Judaism has nothing to do with it, this forces Christians into the compromised position of "talking out of both sides of their mouth," similar to how politicians do. Here's how it works: to remain seeker-friendly and relevant, Christians must appear suspicious and offended by rules and regulations in church. Though they eagerly submit to such rules themselves, they must also appear to be free from and resistant toward the rules, so as to win seekers and nonbelievers. They must project a "no-limits" life of freedom, joy, impact and hope.

It sounds good. It sounds nice ... but it has no teeth, and the proof shows up when those same Christians run afoul of church rules.

Anyone who's ever progressed beyond the status of "seeker" or "nonbeliever" in a church knows – you soon become aware of what is acceptable, and what is forbidden. Christians dress a certain way – usually conservative – and controversies arise when churchgoers flaunt the rules from which they're supposedly set free. Christians refrain from certain uses of language, and avoid certain social situations. Even the most polite, reserved and socially attuned believers wonder (under their breath) why the girl singing on stage wears skin-revealing jeans, midriff tops and shows as much anatomy as she can get away with. The tension is palpable, the person who oversteps the boundaries feels it, and everyone feels guilty and/or ashamed.

Why?

Hasn't the old law has been abolished?

Aren't we free to do as we please?

Why should any of this bother anyone?

Shouldn't we be free to eat what we want, sleep with whomever we please, judge each other on any basis or kill people when they get in our way?

All of that was forbidden by the Torah … but they already told us the Torah no longer applies!

Some Christians attempt to sidestep this issue by claiming that we live "under the law of love" or "under grace." They're fond of citing Jesus' response to the teacher of the law, who asked him, "What is the greatest commandment?"

When the teacher of the law asked that question, Jesus responded, "The greatest commandment is this: 'Hear, O Israel! The LORD our God, the LORD is one. And you shall love the LORD your God with all your heart, soul, mind and strength. And the second is like it: 'You shall love your neighbor as yourself.' Upon these two commandments hang all the law and the prophets."[124]

At the risk of ignoring the Jewish implications of Jesus' answer, most church leaders we've encountered abbreviate this to simply say, "The greatest commandments are to love God with all your heart, soul, mind and strength, and to love your neighbor as yourself."

That sounds simple; love God, love people. A loving person would worship God, and they would not murder, steal, lie, cheat or cause harm to others. Supposedly, it's an open-shut case. You're either loving, or unloving. And for the definition of "love" they turn to the Greek word *agape*, which carries the connotation of "unconditional love." It sounds lovely, like a Hallmark card at

---

[124] Matthew 22:36-40

Christmas. Who could argue with a Father in heaven filled with unconditional love?

Christians also cite Paul's statement in Romans, "We are not under the law, but under grace." We'll go further into depth on this in our forthcoming sequel, The Church In Context. Here's what you need to know in the meantime:

When we hear the English word "love," we assume a certain connotation. We think either of *eros*, which corresponds to romantic love between a man and a woman; of *philia*, meaning "brotherly love," or of *agape* – the unconditional affection of a parent. Most evangelical pastors we've encountered resort to these last two definitions and use the Parable of the Prodigal Son as an example of the latter.[125]

But if you listen to Jewish rabbis speak of love, there's a different connotation, because Jewish rabbis study Biblical Hebrew. In Biblical Hebrew, the word for "love" is *ahav* – and it means neither eroticism, nor unconditional love. Rather, its key connotation is giving – generosity, charity, selflessness and thoughtfulness. Is this similar to unconditional love? In some respects, yes ... but it is not identical to it. This is important – for the simple reason that the God of Israel never interacted with human beings in a one-way relationship where he did all the giving and asked for nothing in return. He always wants something from us, including through Jesus.

---

[125] Luke 15:11-32

Does Jesus demand things from us? You bet he does. He demands our worship, obedience, time, energy, money and self-sacrifice. He demands we do more than obey his commands externally; he desires deep, reformative changes to how we think, speak and choose to feel. His love is good, pure and holy ... but it is hardly guaranteed, in the sense of being freely given without regard to how to we respond. In fact, Jesus devotes a good deal of time in Scripture to warning us of dire consequences for refusing to obey him. That's what we would call a "conditional" relationship. A covenant.

Meanwhile, the phrase "under the law" is an expression for a certain group of people: Gentile converts to Judaism, who underwent circumcision and immersion and voluntarily put themselves "under the law," and then became followers of Jesus when they learned about him. Paul uses the differentiator "under grace" to describe the rest of the Gentile world that remains Gentile, while drawing near to the God of Israel through the sacrifice of Jesus. They did not become Jews, so they are "not under the law, but under grace."

It's worth noting, immediately after Paul said this in Romans 6:14, that he went on to warn Gentiles of the dangers of continuing to sin, didn't he? He warned them of God's judgment. There's another self-canceling statement: there shouldn't be any danger of judgment, if we're not under the law but under grace.

Using this approach, having declared the old law defunct ... Christian leaders then reintroduce portions of the old law, as "the commands of a God who loves us and knows what is best for us." There's nothing objectively false about such statements; Jews believe precisely the same thing about the Torah. God's law is not meant as a punitive or burdensome code, even if some men interpret and enforce it that way. But some Christians hope to escape the accusation of the godless that their faith is a "religion of do's and don'ts." A list of rules for one group of people to control others. We shouldn't be surprised that nonbelievers see through the facade.

Re-Judaizing the Greatest Commandment

Now, let's take another pass at Jesus' answer to the "greatest commandment" question. But this time, let's assume that this is a question from one Jewish rabbi to another, in front of a Jewish audience in First Century Israel.

Firstly, it's important to realize that when you begin with the words "Hear, O Israel," any Jew with a pulse knows exactly what follows. The Sh'ma, one of Israel's most recognized "choruses" – is a prayer almost every Jew knows and recites from memory. To First Century Jews, it was (in some ways) the functional equivalent of the U.S. "Pledge of Allegiance" children once recited every morning before school began. The Sh'ma gets recited 2-3 times per day by observant Jews during the hours of prayer (dawn, 9am, noon, 3pm, dusk). Among other things, it's a check against the ever-present danger of human forgetfulness. The word "Sh'ma" literally translates to "listen and obey," rendering the English word "hear" insufficient to convey the meaning. It is a daily spiritual "alarm clock" to remind the Jews of their duty to obey God.

Jesus quoted these words to the teacher of the law. But if he wanted to tear Israel down and replace Jews with Gentile Christians ... he certainly picked a poor phrase to start. To Jews, the phrase "Sh'ma Yisra'el" is a centerpiece of their unique identity as the people of God. If Jesus was "finished" with Israel and wanted to start a new religion, he should have omitted those words, or changed them to "Hear, O Church!" Instead, he began by reminding everyone present that the greatest commandment is to listen and obey. Not to love ... to listen. And obey.

The fragment "The LORD our God, the LORD is one" always seemed like babble, to me (Paul). In English it sounds like an incomplete sentence: "The LORD is one what?" One person? One spirit? One in a million? One-hit wonder? One flew over the cuckoo's nest? Scripture sometimes seems incredibly vague in English, and that's because English struggles to convey biblical Hebrew. Unlike some other passages Jesus may have spoken in Aramaic, this is one where even poor, uneducated Jews would have understood the Hebrew from all the times they heard it during daily prayers. "Sh'ma, Yisra'el. Adonai Eloheinu. Adonai Echad."

Chasidic Rabbi Manis Friedman points out that when Jews say "God is one," they remind themselves that there is only one reality. One opinion that matters. One force and will that cannot be stopped, overturned, or undone. All human opinions and wills are negotiable and subject to change ... but God's will prevails. Everything that exists and everything that happens does so under that singular reality. The Jew who prays "The LORD is one" reminds himself that no matter what happens, it takes place under the authority and oversight of the God of Israel.

For Jews, this is sometimes a bitter pill to swallow – for that "one reality" therefore extends to include pogroms, persecutions, expulsions, mass murder, gas chambers, ovens, UN resolutions, intifadas, and rocket attacks. From the rising to the setting of the sun, and one end of the universe to the other ... there is only One. There is no other.

Jesus and Paul invoked the idea of "one" as they interacted and reasoned with fellow Jews. When Jesus said, "I and the Father are one,"[126] he wasn't merely saying that he and the Father think the same thoughts or finish each other's sentences. He was telling the Jewish people that their God was in their midst, whether they recognized it or not.

Paul similarly invoked this Hebrew concept when he appealed to Gentile believers in Corinth, concerning foods sacrificed to idols:

"For even if there are so-called gods, whether in heaven or on earth (as indeed there are many "gods" and many "lords"), yet for us there is but one God, the Father, from whom all things came and for whom we live; and there is but one Lord, Jesus Christ, through whom all things came and through whom we live."[127]

The commands to "love the LORD your God with all your heart, soul, and strength" and "love your neighbor as yourself" sound noble and wonderful, to have come from the crusty old legal code of Deuteronomy. Jesus did not pull them out of a hat, or read

---

[126] John 10:30

[127] 1 Corinthians 8:5-6

them off a fortune cookie. He quoted from the Five Books of Moses, written 1500 years before he was born, on that same visit from God to Mount Sinai where he imposed all those (supposedly) harsh rules and restrictions. Why would God keep quoting from his own law if he wants to abolish it? Why would he elevate a passage from a mean-spirited, anachronistic, oppressive rulebook to the position of the "greatest" commandment?

And why do we keep having "commandments," when the commandments are obsolete and burdensome?!

Jesus' final words in this passage: "Upon these two commandments hang all the law and the prophets," also get distorted or misinterpreted. Many Christians we've encountered mistakenly believe, under the false precept that Jesus came to do away with the law, that this statement means "He reduced all 613 commands in the Torah down to just two: 'Love God, and love people.'" Effectively, Jesus canceled the other 611 commandments.

You could compare this to the premise of books like *All I Really Need to Know, I Learned in Kindergarten*. All we really need to do is be nice, kind and loving. That idea works just fine … until it doesn't. I too was taught to be kind and gentle in kindergarten; should I continue to be kind and gentle when an attacker threatens my wife and children? Any man with a family who is worth his salt knows the answer. Jesus is summarizing the Torah, not obliterating it.

Or how about Jesus' own example? Did he always love his neighbor as himself? Did he adhere unerringly to being soft and loving toward people? Not if you were a corrupt Pharisee or a wicked king like Herod! Not if you were a political schemer trying to trick him into making an incriminating statement! Not if you were a money changer in the temple! If you were any of those people, Jesus became a blunt force instrument, throwing his words and weight around like a bull in a china shop. Jesus could get mean, in a holy way. He loved God; he could also be extremely intimidating and fierce.

What if his statement about the rest of the Torah hanging on those two commands simply classified them as "the heart and soul" of the Torah? What if they were the original "source material" for all the other commandments? If that's what he meant, then we're talking in Jewish terms. Judaism lives in constant tension over how the Torah most accurately applies and which laws and commands take precedence over others. Just because those two commands are the greatest doesn't mean they canceled the rest of them.

The "Law" for the Gentiles

The main mistake Gentiles make in listening to church leaders talk about "the old law" is to assume the entire world was once subject to it. To be set "free" from a law, you must first be subject to one. We, for example, cannot be "set free" from the laws of the Central African Republic since neither of us are (or ever have been) citizens or residents of that country. In the same way … at no time in the entire history of Israel did God or the Jewish people ever attempt to compel Gentiles everywhere to be subject to the whole Torah.

Have you noticed that Jews do not evangelize or proselytize the way Christians and Muslims do? That is no accident, nor is it a product of exclusion. Jews keep their spirituality to themselves and serve their fellow human beings through good deeds and acts of charity. Judaism is a way of life, for sure... but it is not a movement like the other two Abrahamic faiths. Judaism makes no attempt to "Judaize" the rest of the world, and most Jews actively discourage Gentiles from trying to do so. Becoming a Jew is, for most Gentiles, "a bridge too far." In Jesus' day, there was significant back-and-forth between rabbis and scholars on whether it even made sense to accommodate Gentiles who wanted to become Jewish.

It's interesting to note that some of God's laws completely predated the existence of the Jews. These laws are known today as "the Noachide laws" because they were given to Noah and his sons after the flood. They constitute seven of the Ten Commandments, and they apply equally to all human beings:

- Worship God

- You shall not worship idols

- You shall not murder

- You shall not steal

- You shall not commit sexual immorality

- You shall not abuse animals

- You shall establish a system of justice

Noah and his sons also received commandments against eating the blood of the animals they slaughtered. So you can see, before the Torah and Mount Sinai, the entire world was under several commandments from God – none of which Christian leaders consider burdensome or old-fashioned.

When the Israelites left Egypt, Moses wrote that "a mixed multitude" went out with them, a collection of tag-alongs from the 70 nations of the world. You might be surprised to learn, according to Jewish tradition, that as much as 80 percent of the Israelites enslaved in Egypt remained in Egypt; the entire Israelite nation never actually left. But along with the Jews who left went a mixed multitude ... of Gentiles. These Gentiles accompanied Israel on its 40-year trek through the wilderness, and some of them lasted a long time. None of them, however, survived to the settling of the Promised Land under Joshua. Nor did any of the older Israelites, except for Joshua and Caleb, the son of Jephunneh.[128]

But that wasn't the end of the matter, because the Jews quickly found themselves making compromises that allowed some Gentiles to remain within their newfound borders. Once the Israelites settled the land, the Torah "fully applied." But even when the Jews occupied the land and set up judges, courts and civil authorities ... there were always parts of the Torah that applied only to certain groups of people, including Gentiles who dwelt among them.

For example, Jewish women freely disregard the commandment of circumcision, while Jewish men ignore purity

---

[128] Numbers 32:11-12

laws concerning menstruation and post-partum. If the Torah requires obedience to all 613 commandments, members of both sexes were/are in immediate non-compliance from the get-go, simply because of gender. So already, we're down from 613 to probably 610, give or take.

Laws forbidding the high priest of Israel from marrying a widow applied only to the high priest; lower-ranking Levites and priests were free to marry widows if they wished. Other laws applied only to Levite priests, but garden-variety Israelites had more leeway. If the Torah requires obedience to all 613 commandments ... 90+ percent of Jews were in immediate non-compliance, merely by virtue of being non-Levites. One site we reviewed, JewFAQ, indicated a total of 29 commandments unique to Levites and priests, which would take that number from 610 to 581.[129]

Several commands in the Torah require the presence of the temple, which has not stood in Jerusalem since it was destroyed by the Romans in the late First Century. Many Levitical sacrifices can only be performed on the temple grounds, using the temple's altars and materials. Others instruct the Jewish people on how to reverence and consecrate the temple. JewFAQ listed 32 distinct commands regarding the temple ... which would further reduce an average Jew's obligations from 581 commands to 549.

Other civil laws could not possibly have been incumbent on all Jewry. The Torah contains seven laws on the proper

---

[129] https://www.jewfaq.org/613_commandments

appointment and behavior of kings. Nine commands regulate the procedure of the Nazirite vow. It has laws that can only be obeyed once, such as the four laws concerning firstborn children and livestock. Six laws govern agriculture and animal husbandry, which would have immediately caused obedience problems for men like Joseph, Jesus' father, whose trade was carpentry. Another 16 laws concerned the Sabbatical and Jubilee years and applied exclusively to the land of Israel – which meant any Jew living outside Israel could not comply. If you stack all these laws together, that's another 42 laws some people could not obey, bringing it down to only 507 laws. (Do you see why these broad brushes don't work?)

It turns out, the Torah is careful to specify when its laws apply only to Jews, versus to both Jews and non-Jews. Usually, you can observe it for yourself, where the text says something like "This law shall apply to the whole nation of Israel, as well as to the foreigner in your midst." God wasn't referring to tourists! From their earliest days in the Promised Land, the Jewish people had Gentiles who lived and worked among them – just as they do today, in modern Israel. Some modern Israeli laws apply no matter who you are, while others do not. For example, modern non-Jews in Israel may work on the Sabbath, but they are not free to disobey Israeli traffic laws. The same principle is at work.

The Torah was the underlying framework of the four prohibitions by the Jerusalem Council in Acts 15. This is obvious because (a) they mirror both the Noachide laws and the Torah, and (b) no contemporary Gentile societies had such laws. The council told Gentile believers to abstain from food sacrificed to idols (idolatry), eating strangled animals (cruelty to animals), eating blood, and sexual immorality.[130]

The apostles did not pick those prohibitions out of a Cracker Jack box! They mentioned them in reaction to the habits and customs of the pagan societies where their disciples lived. Rome, Greece, and the rest of the European, African and Middle Eastern (pagan) nations where the Jews spread, especially after the destruction of Jerusalem. Lands where Gentiles in particular would face pressure to eat foods and participate in idolatrous festivals. It's absurd to suggest those commands came from anywhere but Judaism.

The Jerusalem Council simply reinforced what Jews and Gentiles had always observed, to live together peaceably in Israel. The difference was that Israel was spreading across the globe, because it now extended (in a commonwealth sense) to any Gentile who accepted Jesus as the Messiah.

For the rest of the Torah, the tradition in Israel was that it did not apply to Gentiles.

But if Jesus was the promised Jewish Messiah, who brought "the nations" (Gentiles) close to the God of Israel … what did that mean for those Gentiles, from a "legal" perspective?

We know, from the volumes of argument in the New Testament, that Paul adamantly disagreed with the suggestion the Gentiles had to become fully Jewish to be saved. It's also clear,

---

[130] Acts 15:22-29

from prophecies like Isaiah 56, that God desires to be the God of both Jews and non-Jews. He wants people from every tribe, tongue and nation in his kingdom. In the book of Revelation, he made clear to the apostle John that the "mixed multitude" of the kingdom will be a gigantic melting pot. Frankly, we believe it would go against God's character to have a monochromed, monolithic, homogeneous group of people in eternity. How boring would that be!

On the other hand, if God desires Gentiles in his kingdom … how do you think he wants us to behave once we're admitted? From all this time and effort he spends teaching Jews how to live, wouldn't you think he wants Gentiles to develop a similar inner compass?

Let's think of it another way: when you became a Christian, did your life draw closer to the Torah? Or did your presence cause the Torah to slap its forehead, realize how much more enlightened and morally upright you were, and reform itself?

We would wager that your life drew closer to the Torah. You got baptized, began attending church, started paying tithes, attended Bible studies and life groups, and sought a relationship with the God of Israel. You became aware of sin and took pains to turn away from your former life. Your life became more aligned with and observant of Torah, even if you wouldn't use those words to describe it.

So … did Jesus provide a "Torah" for Gentiles?

We believe so.

There are two. Primary among them are the writings of Paul, who declared himself "an apostle to the Gentiles" in Romans 11, the section of that letter that unpacks how Gentiles are "grafted in" to the commonwealth of Israel.[131] In contrasting himself with Peter, the "apostle to the Jews," Paul made clear that Jesus charged him with the responsibility of spreading the gospel to non-Jews. But in that same section, Paul also told Gentile readers that they should not take their "graftedness" lightly. He made no suggestion whatsoever that God abolished or retired the Torah; if anything, his encouragement toward Gentiles is that they learn to live and behave like their Jewish brothers and sisters while maintaining their cultural identity. They were to be "Gentiles who lived as Jews," presenting themselves as living sacrifices and conducting their daily lives with reverence, submission, and cheerful obedience to Jewish precepts (without sacrificing their non-Jewish identities).

This is how I (Paul) live my life: though I do have a smattering of Jewish ancestry, I consider myself a Gentile ... who lives like a Jew.

This does not mean I wear a kippah, put on tefillin, or sew tzitzit onto the corners of my garments. That would be inauthentic because I am an uncircumcised, distant physical descendant of Abraham. Instead, as Paul (the apostle) would say, I am "a Jew inwardly."[132] My heart is circumcised and oriented toward a Jewish approach to work, worship, and rest. I study the Jewish Scriptures with a rabbi and utter predominantly Jewish prayers. I speak, write,

---

[131] Romans 11:11-24

[132] Romans 2:29

and study Biblical Hebrew. I read extrabiblical literature, such as the Sayings of the Fathers, the Talmud, and the Mishnah. I make friends with Jews of all stripes and try to learn from them. I observe the Appointed Times – Passover, Shavuot, Yom Teruah, Yom Kippur, and Sukkot. I also fast or observe Jewish days of remembrance in solidarity with the nation of Israel. The term "Messianic Gentile" recently emerged in Messianic Jewish thought; it is a title I embrace.

The second piece of evidence from apostolic lore is "The Didache," attributed to the apostles (though never canonized in Scripture). Its original title is "The Teaching of the Lord to the Gentiles Through the Twelve Apostles." It consists of just one book, with 16 chapters, and perhaps 160 verses. The Didache is an effective paraphrase of the Torah, helping Gentiles orient themselves to life in the kingdom alongside Jews – but without forcing them to engage in centuries of catch-up to understand the entire Jewish universe.

In the twelve words of its original title, the Didache makes clear that the Jewish apostles and believers distinguished between themselves and Gentiles. A teaching "to the Gentiles" would not have been necessary among a group of believers where no such distinction existed. The Didache's content, in parallel fashion, prescribes a more straightforward, concise code of appropriate living for Gentiles. Take, for example, its flexibility toward and recognition of the complicated nature of immersion (baptism):

Concerning immersion, immerse in this way:

Having first said all these things, immerse in the name of the Father, the Son, and the Holy Spirit in living water.

But if you do not have living water, immerse in other water; if you cannot immerse in cold water, then immerse in warm water.

But if you do not have either in sufficient quantity to immerse, pour water on the head three times in the name of the Father and the Son and the Holy Spirit.

Prior to the immersion, the one performing the immersion and the one being immersed should fast beforehand, and also any others if they can. Require the one being immersed to fast one or two days prior to the immersion.

This reveals that Jews typically prescribed certain sources, temperatures and quantities of water for an immersion to take place. The text shows a healthy respect and empathy for the limitations of Gentiles in the corners of the world where they lived. Most societies did not build mikvahs, and none had a rite like immersion. Much of the world's Gentile population lived a much greater distance than Jews did from "living" waters like the Sea of Galilee, the Mediterranean Sea, or the Jordan River; their closest water source might have been a local well. Some dwelt in dry, hot deserts where water was very sparse; others in remote, frigid regions where most water was frozen solid for several months per year. The apostles recognized that demanding Jewish levels of obedience from Gentiles was absurd, particularly since so many of them lived outside the land of Israel and away from the temple.

But the biggest reason the Didache simplifies obedience for Gentiles is the consequences of their decision to follow Jesus – stigma, social censure, ostracism, persecution, or even imprisonment and death. Unlike the Jewish believers, Gentiles who chose Jesus incurred suspicion, hostility, and tremendous personal fallout from their native pagan cultures. Rome branded Gentile followers of Jesus as "atheists."

Modern Western readers might wonder, "What's the big deal? This is the Roman Empire! You don't need to go far to find a river, stream or lake."

But there we go again – retrojecting onto First Century believers modern freedoms of movement we take for granted, as well as Anglo-American social niceties of "minding one's own business" and "live and let live."

Only in the last few years, at the time of writing, have we begun a return to pagan traditions of "social credits" in the fallout from massive events like COVID-19. If you incurred rage and hostility during those years for wearing / not wearing facemasks, for example ... now you have a taste of what it's like to live in a godless, pagan society where your entire character (and fate) gets judged by whether you check all the right boxes. Now you know the bitter roots of division that led to the baseless hatred among and between the Jews themselves, before and during Jesus' time. Now, perhaps, you understand why the apostles made efforts to avoid stonewalling Gentiles who came into the Kingdom of God.

Despite all this, the Jewish authors of the Didache remained steadfastly committed to the idea that immersion was very much a rite of integration into Judaism and a Jewish lifestyle. Contrary to Christianity's adaptation, immersion was a regular Jewish activity that the believer engaged anytime they drifted, committed sins or lost their connection with God, or chose to more fully apply themselves to faith. This explains the emphasis on fasting, for all the participants. In this context, fasting is an activity closely associated with repentance, just as Jesus fasted during his 40 days in the wilderness, during the season of Teshuvah. The Jews also fast for their transgressions on Yom Kippur, the highest holy day, where the Divine Council gathers to render judgments on every living being.

So ... did Jesus set Gentiles "free" from the law?

We submit that it's the other way around; rather than setting Gentiles "free" from the law, he actually brought us under it. (Albeit in a manner different from the one characterized by the biblical expression "under the law," meaning "conversion to becoming Jewish.")

The correct answer is a double-headed rhetorical question:

"How can you be 'set free' from laws you were never obligated to obey, even while dutifully obeying others you claim you're 'free' from having to obey?"

You may as well ask whether either of us (the authors) were "set free" from English Common Law, which influences and governs both the United States and New Zealand to this day. Even then, the answer is ... "Sort of. It depends."

Both of us can be called as witnesses, under the penalty of perjury, to testify in courts of law in the US and New Zealand. Those are features of the English traditions of jurisprudence, enforced by judiciaries set up by the British authorities that established both of the nations where we live. Are we, therefore, bound to English Common Law?

We suppose so! If we give false testimony in American or Kiwi courts, we can be punished under perjury laws that originated in Great Britain (who stole them from Israel).

But do we have to pay taxes to the British Crown, or kneel when English royalty pays a visit to our countries? Of course not. Now, suddenly, we are "free" from English Common Law ... even as we are also bound to it.

The same is true for Gentiles, grafted into the Commonwealth of Israel. God gave the seven Noachide laws to Gentiles, before Jews existed, in the immediate aftermath of the Flood. Those laws also made it into the canon of the Ten Commandments, which God gave to the Jewish people. They also survived into present-day Christianity, which we can easily discern from the reactions of Christian churches and leaders when someone violates them. So in a sense, we have always been "bound" to some of God's commands, and we always will be.

God gave the Jewish people 613 total commandments in the Torah. But at no time has there ever been an individual Jew responsible to keep all 613 of them, for the simple reason that they don't all apply equally to everyone. Some apply only to men, some only to women, some to Levites and priests, some to kings, some concern only the temple, some to ordinary Jewish citizens of both sexes, and some to people of all backgrounds, no matter their gender — but only if they live in the land of Israel.

As for Christians, there are over one thousand commands in the gospels and apostolic writings.[133] That's hardly a paragon of liberality and permissiveness, wouldn't you say? If you're going to assert that Jesus' death "set Christians free" from the Torah, you might do well to ask, "How come we still have to follow all these rules? And who came up with them?"

The truest, most hopeful answer we can find is that the apostles neither rescinded Torah, nor did they add to it. There's no "new" command, not even when Jesus says "Behold, I give you a new command: love one another." Guess what? The command "love one another"? That's also in the Torah! As Rabbi Matt Rosenberg likes to point out, Jesus said "nothing new." That's why he cried out "Repent!" instead of "Revolt!" His mission was always to return people to the original worship and obedience of the God of Israel.

The Punishment is Settled, Not the Law

There's one more problem, however. What about passages in the writings of Paul that seem to indicate the opposite? For one simple example, let's take this one: "Christ redeemed us from the curse of the law by becoming a curse for us; for it is written,

---

[133] https://www.abc.net.au/reslib/201407/r1308729_17984331.pdf

'Cursed is everyone who is hung on a tree.'"[134] That sounds straightforward, doesn't it? Let's put it in bullets:

A. The law was a curse

B. Christ redeemed us from the curse by becoming a curse for us

C. Because the law says so

Do you see the obvious problem? You can't have "A" and "B" without "C" ... but if "C" is itself a curse you wish to get rid of, how can it also be an authoritative source?

That would be like saying, "The President of the United States pardoned all incarcerated Americans from their sentences by sentencing himself to prison in their stead because the law says, 'People who break the law shall be subject to imprisonment.' Even though, at the same time, the law no longer applies."

What sort of talk is that?! Let's try it one more time:

The President of the United States ...

... responsible for enforcing the laws ...

... pardons all convicted felons by sentencing himself to prison ...

... because the law says that people who break the law should go to prison ...

---

[134] Galatians 3:13

... even though the law is canceled.

Come again?!

That's quite a non-sequitur statement. If the law is canceled, neither the felons nor the president should go to prison, and certainly not "because the law says so."

So, could Paul have meant something other than the Torah when he used the word "curse"?

Yes ... if his writings are those of a Jewish rabbi, writing mainly to other Jews, in First Century Jewish Diaspora.

Because to Jews, the "curse" of the law is not the same as the law itself. That seems more sensible, doesn't it? If the Torah is itself a curse, it wouldn't be necessary to say "Cursed is everyone who hangs on a tree." Why? Well, because you don't have to hang on a tree to be subject to Torah. You just have to be born Jewish, and the Torah automatically applies, beginning (for baby boys) on Day 8 of your life. If that were the case, it should read, "Cursed is everyone born as a Jew."

But that isn't what Moses said ... it's not what he meant ... it's not what Paul said, and it's not what he meant either!

So what did he mean when he said that Christ "redeemed us from the curse of the law"?

Paul quoted (again) from the Torah, despite his supposed determination to undermine and abolish it. It's funny how he kept contradicting himself and quoting from a series of books he supposedly considered rubbish.

So what does the passage, taken from Deuteronomy, actually say?

"If someone guilty of a capital offense is put to death and their body is exposed on a tree, you must not leave the body hanging on the tree overnight. Be sure to bury it that same day, because anyone who is hung on a tree is under God's curse."[135]

Do you notice the words "capital offense"?

The "curse" of the Torah is not the Torah itself … rather, it is the punishment for disobeying it, at the level of a capital offense!

In other words, Paul told the Galatians that Christ redeemed us from the punishment of disobeying the Torah, not the Torah itself! Now that's good news, especially for Gentiles.

It means that Jesus did indeed sacrifice himself on our behalf, and became the "punishment" for our disobedience.

It means that we, who spent our pre-Kingdom lives living any old way we choose, can come near to the God of Israel by virtue of Jesus' heroic sacrifice, and be redeemed from the "curse" (punishment) of breaking Torah — the (Noachide) parts of the Torah to which all of humanity was bound after the Flood.

---

[135] Deuteronomy 21:22-23

Christian Interpretation	Jewish Interpretation
God gave the law through Moses on Mount Sinai, and it was binding upon all human beings everywhere	God originally gave the first seven laws to Noah after the Flood for all humanity; he later offered the Torah to all humanity, but only Israel accepted it. The rest of the nations went their own way, according to their own laws and customs.
When the law is in force, it applies to all human beings equally, in any and every situation	Some Torah laws apply universally, while others apply only to certain people – men, women, priests, Levites, kings, and foreigners
The apostles decided to drop the law's requirements for Gentiles because they themselves knew how much trouble the Jews had in keeping it	The apostles declined to enforce full compliance with the law for Gentiles because they knew: (a) the difficulty Gentiles would have in understanding it (b) full adoption of Jewish law would erase their Gentile identity (c) they would undermine Scripture and prophecy if they became Jews
Jesus set us free from the law by becoming a curse, under the authority of the law he'd already canceled	Jesus set us free from the punishment for disobeying the law by becoming a curse, according to the law

Now you might say, "Well, I'm innocent! I've never murdered, stolen, lied, cheated, committed sexual immorality, abused animals, eaten blood or worshiped idols."

If so, we congratulate you on such a sterling record. We hope it holds up for you in the courtrooms of the Divine Council. It is possible to live a very upright and virtuous life, for most of your years, under the right circumstances. We sincerely hope your humility outpaces your obedience and conformity, to the point you eagerly join in building God's Kingdom here on earth. There are such things as people with abundantly good, kind, gentle and humble natures ... just not very many of them.

But you'll have to reckon with Jesus' definitions of murder, theft, dishonesty, sexual immorality, animal abuse and idol worship. Those are much more difficult to pass flawlessly, and we encourage you to consider that perhaps you've "forgotten" some of the times you transgressed, however slight or inconsequential. It is Jesus who promises that each person will be held to full account for every single word they spoke and action they took.[136] But by all means, if you feel confident you can persuade him of your squeaky-cleanness ... don't let us stop you.

For everyone else, as they say, there's Mastercard.

---

[136] Matthew 12:36

CONCLUSION

Westerners often remark that "the devil is in the details" — and we have found that so does the God of Israel. You've probably noticed how much detail, analysis and rigor goes into understanding the text. That too is a Jewish way of reading and studying it.

But the Jewish approach to reading Scripture goes way beyond "just slowing down." You have to understand the quirks and characteristics of the authors, as well as the four traditional ways of reading, so you can discern when a Bible author is speaking plainly, versus when he's making a veiled reference to Jewish thoughts, ideas, legends or lore.

And of course, you'll miss volumes of detail by continuing to read in English. Hebrew is far beyond "just another human language." The Jews call it "The Lord's Language," and when you begin to understand its mathematical, pictographic and mystical brilliance … you'll see how poorly English measures up.

To illustrate some of the difficulty, here's a loose parallel contained in the lyrics of the song called "Song For Another Time," by American country artists Old Dominion:

So before we're singing 'I Will Always Love You'
Let's sing 'Brown-Eyed Girl,' 'Sweet Caroline'
'Free Fall,' 'Small Town Saturday Night'
Before you lose 'That Loving Feeling'
Let's go 'Dancing on the Ceiling'
Keep on living that 'Teenage Dream'

'Paradise City' where the grass is green

Pretty soon you'll be 'Always On My Mind'

But that's a song for another time

If you grew up listening to the popular music of the 1960s through to today, you recognize these lyrics as the titles of other popular songs. They're references to previous works, which the singer uses to describe his intent toward the subject of his song (a woman). He's using them as shorthand "hints" — saying what he wants to say poetically, without resorting to everyday language. In plain-spoken English, this might go:

So before you leave me

Let me tell you how beautiful you are

Let's go out and party recklessly in this small town where we live

Before we break up and you leave me

Let's go out dancing and feel like we're in love

Let's have sex one more time

Let's live like there's no tomorrow and pursue pleasure at all costs

Very soon you'll be a bittersweet memory in my soul

But I can deal with that later

You could read Old Dominion's lyrics to most members of our generation who grew up in the West, and they'd recognize at least a few of the titles. Music nerds like us recognize nearly all of them, and can discern their meaning.

But if you read those same titles to Westerners 200 years from now, they would consider the lyrics anachronistic and irrelevant. They would have no idea what the words refer to, and it wouldn't matter to them because they'd be busy celebrating 23rd Century popular music.

Which is precisely why it's not enough to read the Bible slowly, particularly if you're reading in English. It requires a Jewish mind steeped in the Hebrew language, biblical discipleship and the history of Israel to point out what you'll miss.

Hence, you too will need a rabbi to continue your journey.

ACKNOWLEDGMENTS

Doron

First and foremost, I need to say "Baruch Hashem" to the God of my fathers, Abraham, Isaac, and Jacob, for allowing me to be a "Levite" in His temple. It is my joy and honour to be a vessel of the temple like my ancestors.

To my wife who daily lives the Jesus I teach about; to my children, Nathan, Holly and Benjamin, who I pray will embrace their Jewishness for the sake of Jesus and my abba and ima, who always knew I had to be doing what I am doing. As I always say to you, my success is your success and to my siblings and their partners who also allow me to be the spiritual leader in our family, I see your service and acceptance.

To those who have over the years and will over the coming years, trust me enough to listen to what I have to say in the name of Yeshua, know that I pray for you all daily. I do not take for granted the magnitude of the responsibility I have in ministry. Every day I pray the Amidah. I mention you all when I think of the "righteous converts". I know for those of you who have been on the online platforms where I type endlessly, that you have effectively already read volumes of books if they were to be published. Thank you for enduring me!

To my co-author, Paul. I could write a book just thanking Hashem for the value you have brought to the ministry and this project. I feel a level of confidence with your help that I never imagined possible. You know how I go on in praise when we speak about this. Todah rabah.

To Jason, of Emissary Publishing, alongside Paul. Thank you for your generosity in being willing to educate me on the professional publishing/editing processes and for allowing your experience and resourcing to be channeled for this project.

To every reader who may pick up this book, I just want to invite you to approach this book with a healthy dose of skepticism. I don't mind if you approach with a level of "apprehension", that is responsible. All I ask in addition to that is that you allow your own worldview to be approached with a similar level of skepticism for the sake of preserving truth, not opinion.

As I say to my students… "Let the evidence convince you…"

Paul

To the Holy One, blessed be He – You are too kind and generous to a man who has done You so very many wrongs. May this work bless Your people and open their eyes a little wider, as You opened mine.

To my bride, Shannon, and my sons, Grant and Chase – may God make you fruitful, like Ephraim, Manasseh, Rachel and Leah. Thank you for being you.

To Doron – Mazel Tov, my friend, my rabbi. Having you in my life is like having my uncle back. Peace and joy reign supreme when we draw near to the light. Let there be light.

To the men of my Torah Club – David, Herb, Dion, Alan, Andy, Colin, Jeff, Jacek – thank you for pre-reading (and pre-reading again!) It is good and holy to break bread with you every week over Torah.

To the crew in our yeshiva, On The Way – Caleb Wilson, Jesse, Dana, Doug, Joash, Caleb Murphy, Gary, Conrad, Dianne, Nande, Tiffany, Alona, Jo … who am I missing? Keep learning and keep growing! Mazel Tov!

To Kano Kinnaman, my dear friend, who sharpens me all the time as we discuss Torah and various other topics on our Shabbat chat.

To the kindest of Jewish friends I've had the pleasure of learning from – Shana Forta, Rabbi Yonason Goldson, Rabbi Daniel & Susan Lapin … it's unlikely you'll read this, but you helped me grow as a believer nonetheless.

To my business partner, Jason Todd, who forced me to do a better job of explaining and only using sarcasm as a last resort! Also an incredible strategist, designer and partner-in-crime for telling the stories that matter at Emissary Publishing!

To my Christian friends who read what I write, and don't walk away just because it's challenging or makes you think – Clarence Montgomery, Evan Money, Joe Lewis, Eric Bucher, Leon

Scamahorn, Cory Sexton, Scott Hooper … there are more, I know. We're on the same team! Thank you for putting up with my fastidiousness and obsession with language.

Jude 24-25

www.ingramcontent.com/pod-product-compliance
Lightning Source LLC
Chambersburg PA
CBHW060517130626
46553CB00002B/534

* 9 7 9 8 9 9 0 5 5 6 2 3 2 *